WHO HELPED HITLER?

By the same author

BEFORE THE STORM
JOURNEY INTO THE PAST

IVAN MAISKY

Soviet Ambassador to the United Kingdom, 1932–43,
Member of the Academy of Sciences of the U.S.S.R.

*

WHO HELPED HITLER?

Translated from the Russian by
ANDREW ROTHSTEIN

HUTCHINSON OF LONDON

HUTCHINSON & CO. (*Publishers*) LTD
178–202 Great Portland Street, London, W.1

London Melbourne Sydney
Auckland Bombay Toronto
Johannesburg New York

First published in Russia as
KTO POMOGAL GITLERU

(Izdatelstvo Instituta Mezhdunarodnykh
Otnoshenii; Moscow 1962)

This edition: First published 1964

*This book has been set in Fournier type face. It has
been printed in Great Britain by The Anchor Press,
Ltd., in Tiptree, Essex, on Antique Wove paper.*

CONTENTS

FOREWORD

THE enemies of the U.S.S.R. abroad have brought into being and spread far and wide a spurious legend about the behaviour of the Soviet Government on the very eve of the second world war. The essence of this legend is the following.

It is asserted that in the spring and summer of 1939 (from March to August) the Soviet Union was playing a double game: on the one hand it was carrying on open negotiations with Britain and France for the conclusion of a triple pact of mutual assistance for the struggle against Hitlerite Germany, while on the other hand, behind the backs of Britain and France, it carried on parallel but secret negotiations with Hitlerite Germany for the conclusion of an agreement aimed at the 'western democracies'. It is alleged, further, that the Soviet Union by seizing on various unessential details artificially dragged out negotiations with Britain and France, awaiting the end of its talks with Germany, and that when, nevertheless, the moment came for signing the triple pact, it suddenly changed its attitude altogether, broke with Britain and France and concluded an agreement with Germany— an agreement which (usually this is mentioned in deliberately vague terms) was practically a military alliance directed against Britain and France. Our enemies, finally, allege that the signature of this agreement between the Soviet Union and Germany opened the way for Hitler's attack on Poland, and that thereby the responsibility for launching the second world war falls on the U.S.S.R.

7

This malicious legend, originated in 1939–40, was systematically worked up after the war and filled out with all kinds of details, was reproduced in numerous alternative versions and received wide publicity at the hands of western politicians, journalists and historians. It found its way even into the most responsible diplomatic documents of the capitalist governments, including the notes of Mr. Eisenhower, former President of the U.S.A.

Yet this legend is a classic example of the bourgeois falsification of history, based on the calculation that the mass of the people have a short memory and are little acquainted with the true facts of international relations. The falsification was a double one. In the first place, the events themselves—in the spring and summer of 1939—were crudely distorted. Secondly, they were taken in isolation, detached from the past out of which they developed—while such a representation of events prevents their proper understanding and evaluation. And in order to 'sell', as the Americans say, this falsification more easily to a wide public, its authors usually avoided a detailed account of the history of the tripartite negotiations, and preferred to speak of them in general terms, briefly, summarily, without details, alleging that it was 'generally known'—a proposition not requiring proof—that the Soviet Union bore the blame for the collapse of the negotiations.

In the pages that follow I shall tell the real truth about what actually did take place in the relations between the U.S.S.R. and Britain, France and Germany in the spring and summer of 1939. I have particular advantages in performing this task. On the one hand, as Soviet Ambassador in London in those days, I was a witness of and a participant in the tripartite negotiations of 1939 between the U.S.S.R., Britain and France. On the other hand, as a historian in the post-war period, I was able to study all the literature (documents, memoirs, monographs, etc.) about the eve of the second world war, published after it was over.

However, in order that the truth which I shall set forth should be the real truth, I must begin my account not with 1939 but from a much earlier date. That date naturally is determined by the point which was a watershed in the era between the two wars: the coming to power of Hitlerism in Germany.

Such a date for the beginning of the story is also very convenient for myself. I decided to present my account in the form of reminiscences because such a form would convey to the reader more easily the atmosphere and the events of those already comparatively far-off years. Also I arrived in London as Ambassador of the U.S.S.R. in the autumn of 1932: that is, only three months before the Nazi coup in Berlin.

Thus both political and personal considerations make it particularly convenient to begin my account with the first impressions I gained immediately upon my arrival in Britain.

Although the events to be discussed in the following pages took place more than a quarter of a century ago, they have a lively echo in the events of the present day.

For then, just as today, the international political horizon was wrapped in heavy thunder-clouds. Then, as now, the fundamental problem facing humanity was the problem of whether there was or was not to be a new world war. Then, as now, the camp of Socialism, represented in those days only by the Soviet Union, was defending the cause of peace with all its strength, while the camp of capitalism, which at that time included all the other countries and States, was blindly and criminally hurtling to war, and in the end led humanity into a terrible catastrophe. When one listens now to the speeches of the present leaders of capitalism one often thinks: Chamberlain and Daladier used to say the same things in the thirties. Evidently the sons have learned nothing from the experience of their fathers.

But does this mean that things must end once more in a new and still more frightful world war?

No, it does not. During the twenty-odd years which have passed since then, the balance of power in the international arena has completely changed.

At that time the U.S.S.R. was the only Socialist State on our planet. Today there is an entire constellation of such States,

including the mighty Chinese People's Republic. Under the red
banner of Socialism over one-third of all mankind has taken its
stand in our day. Another third is constituted by the neutral
States, which are also champions of peace and opponents of war.
In the camp of militant capitalism there now remains only about
one-third of mankind, and within that one-third there are more
than a few friends of peace. It is just that relationship of forces in
the international arena which gives us grounds for considering
that a third world war is not by any means inevitable, and that
with the necessary activity and energy displayed by the forces of
peace it can be averted.

In such a situation it is useful to recall what took place on the
eve of the second world war. It is particularly important to
demonstrate the phenomenal and historic blindness of the then
governments of the Western Powers, who did not see and did
not want to see the abyss into which they were dragging mankind
—a blindness which followed from their hatred of Communism
and the Soviet State. A clear picture of that blindness, and of the
fatal consequences to which it led, may help the wiser elements in
the present-day capitalist camp to learn the lessons of the recent
past, and thereby help the victory of the forces of peace over the
forces of war.

                                                    IVAN MAISKY

PART ONE

Before 1939

I

The Soviet Government's instructions

IN THE autumn of 1932 I was appointed Ambassador of the
U.S.S.R. to Great Britain, and at the end of October that year,
after the British Government had given its *agrément*, I left for
London.

What tasks did the Soviet Government put before me? With
what intentions, plans and feelings did I leave for the place of
my new work?

I can say safely that the Soviet Government was sending me as
a herald of peace and friendship between the U.S.S.R. and Great
Britain, and I myself gladly and willingly set about the fulfilment
of such a mission. By no means over-estimating my own forces, I
decided beforehand to do everything possible to improve relations
between Moscow and London. The reasons underlying the aims
of the Soviet Government were both general and particular in
their character.

The reasons of a more general character sprang from the
inherently peaceful nature of the Soviet State, where there are
no classes or groups which might gain anything from war.
Workers, peasants and intellectuals—the social elements of which
the Soviet community consists—can only lose by war. This, of
course, does not in the least mean that they are for peace at any
price. The Bolsheviks are not Tolstoyans. As the well-known
Soviet song runs our 'armoured train' is always ready on the
sidings, maintained at the level of the most up-to-date military
technique: and, should the Soviet State be in peril, it is immediately brought, and will be brought, into operation. But *in our
essence* we do not want war, we hate war and to the extent of

human possibility we try to avoid war. We are wholly engaged in the building of Socialism and Communism; it is here that our minds and hearts are committed, and we wish for nothing which could distract us from this work we ardently desire or which, all the more, could seriously interfere with it. Such always was, and is today, the general line of the Soviet State. If, nevertheless, the U.S.S.R. during its forty-five years of history has had to do a great deal of fighting, this was due to the fact that *war was imposed on us by hostile external forces*, which were striving to wipe from the face of the earth the first Socialist country in the world. That is how it was during the years of the Civil War and foreign intervention. That is how it was in the days of the great Patriotic War of 1941–5.

The reasons of a more particular character which still further impelled the Soviet Government to live in peace and friendship with Great Britain at the time of my appointment as Ambassador in London, consisted, on the one hand, in some special features of the internal situation in our country, and on the other in the rapidly growing menace of Fascism in Germany.

I will deal first with the internal situation in the U.S.S.R. When I left for Britain the first Five Year Plan was drawing to a close. The foundations for our new industry had been laid, but the fruits of the heroic efforts which they cost were a matter for the future. Collective farming had only just been born, and the struggle of the kulaks against it was not yet over. The country was experiencing difficulties with foodstuffs. There were insufficient consumer goods. Beyond the boundaries of the U.S.S.R there was raging a cruel economic crisis (the notorious crisis of 1929–33). World prices for foodstuffs and raw materials, by the export of which in the main we were paying in those years for the machines imported from abroad, had fallen seriously. Income in foreign currency was small. The Soviet gold industry was still going through the first stages of its regeneration after the destruction caused by the Civil War and intervention, and was in no way helped by the management of the Lena goldfields by foreign concessionaires in the twenties. As a result, it was extremely

difficult to keep up regular payments for the industrial equipment imported from abroad. I can remember really critical
moments in the winter of 1932-3 when I was already working in
London. However, the Soviet Government always paid on the
day and hour appointed. We valued highly the reputation
established on the world market by the U.S.S.R. for meeting its
obligations without fail, and spared no efforts to preserve it. All
this, naturally, impelled the Soviet Government to avoid any
external political complications which might create difficulties for
our trade and arouse the necessity for unforeseen expenditure.

This was not only a noble policy but also an extremely wise
one, but how difficult it was to maintain it in those years!

Turning to Germany, at the end of 1932 the Weimar Republic
was visibly in a state of complete collapse. The Nazis were rapidly
gaining, conquering one position after another. The split in the
ranks of the proletariat was profound, and the Social-Democrats
were stubbornly refusing any co-operation with the Communists
against Fascism. In such a situation it was extremely probable
that Hitler would come to power—and if that should happen,
what would be its effect on the whole European situation? How
in particular would it be reflected in German-Soviet relations?
Nothing good, of course, could be expected of such an outcome.

Before leaving for London I had a long talk with M. M.
Litvinov, then People's Commissar for Foreign Affairs, in which
he gave me the general directions for the work I was to do in
Britain.

'You understand, of course,' explained Maxim Maximovich,
'that these are not my personal views, but the directives of our
higher authorities.'

That conversation I remember very well, and think it desirable
to reproduce its most important points here.

'Soviet foreign policy,' said M. M. Litvinov, 'is a policy of
peace. This follows from our principles and from the very
foundations of the Soviet State. The basis of our foreign policy
never changes, but in putting it into practical effect we have to
reckon with the particular international situation prevailing. Up

to now our best relations have been with Germany, and in our
actions we have tried as far as possible to maintain a united front
with Germany, or at any rate to take her position and her interests
into account. But the Germany with which we were dealing was
Weimar Germany. Today that Germany is visibly on its last legs.
We cannot cherish any illusions in that respect. If not today, then
tomorrow Hitler will come to power, and the situation will
change at once. Germany will be transformed from our friend
into our enemy. If that is the prospect, what conclusion must we
draw? Obviously now, in the interests of our policy of peace, we
must try to improve our relations with Britain and France—
particularly with Britain as the leading Power in capitalist
Europe. True, both these States up to now have been hostile to
us. . . .'

To illustrate this point Maxim Maximovich recalled some of
the most important facts: the leading part played by Britain and
France in the intervention of 1918–20, the Curzon ultimatum of
1923, the raid on Arcos and the rupture of Anglo-Soviet
diplomatic relations in 1927, the frenzied anti-Soviet campaigns of
1930–1. He continued:

'But now the objective world situation is changing. The Nazis
when they come to power will of course raise a frightful noise for
a war of revenge: they will begin to arm, to demand the
restoration of their colonies and so forth. This is bound to make
the ruling circles of Britain and France see reason, if only
partially, and must compel them to think of allies against
Germany. Then they will be obliged to remember the Entente of
the war years, and consequently our country. This will create
a more favourable situation for your work in London. But you
cannot rely much on things developing on their own. Your task
will be to make the greatest use of the situation coming into being
in Britain, in the interests of Anglo-Soviet *rapprochement*.'

'I agree with your assessment of the situation and your
conclusions,' I said, 'but what do you conceive to be the immediate practical steps?'

'I will speak now only about your mission in England,' he

replied. 'What must you strive for first of all? The extension in every possible way of our ties with the Conservatives. Two forces are dominant in the political life of Great Britain—the Conservatives and the Opposition, consisting of Labour and the Liberals. Once the Liberals played first fiddle in the Opposition, but those times are gone. In our days the Liberals are declining, splitting, weakening. The main role in the Opposition is passing more and more to the Labour Party. You should note that up to now all the positive steps in the sphere of Anglo-Soviet relations have come from the Liberals or from Labour. Thus, for example, the first and very important trade agreement between Britain and Soviet Russia in 1921 was signed by a Government led by Lloyd George. Diplomatic recognition of the U.S.S.R. in 1924 was effected by the first Labour Government. The restoration of diplomatic relations between the two countries, broken off in 1927, was brought about by the second Labour Government in 1929. On the contrary, so far we have seen only hostile actions by the Conservatives. This is a pity, because, after all, the Conservatives have been and remain the bosses in Britain. And so long as the Conservatives do not change their attitude, our relations with Britain will remain unstable and subject to all kinds of chance unpleasantness.'

Maxim Maximovich adjusted a pile of papers on the desk in front of him and concluded:

'In London we have had, and still have, good relations with Labour: you should cultivate these relations in every possible way, they are very important, particularly having future prospects in mind. We have not bad relations with some groups of the Liberals: take every step to strengthen and widen them. But among the Conservatives we have scarcely any contacts at all. Yet I repeat that they are the real bosses in Britain! Therefore your very first and most important task is to break through the icy wall which separates our London Embassy from the Conservatives, and establish the widest and most reliable contacts possible with them. If you succeed in this, it will be a useful step in the struggle against German aggression. Think out your most

B

immediate steps after your arrival in London and let me know them: then we shall have another talk.'

Two days later I again visited the People's Commissar, and told him of the programme of initial activities in Britain which I had drawn up. It amounted to the following three main points:

1. Immediately after presenting my credentials I give an interview to the British press.

2. I extend as widely as possible the series of visits which diplomatic etiquette imposes on a newly appointed Ambassador, and in doing so cover not only the narrow circle of persons connected with the Foreign Office but also a number of members of the Government, prominent politicians, people of the City and representatives of the cultural world.

3. I lay particular stress on the problem of expanding Anglo-Soviet trade.

M. M. Litvinov approved my plans, and asked whether I had prepared the text of my press interview. I handed him my draft. He read it through, made a few minor textual corrections and then approved it in its final form. The statement read:

'In entering on the fulfilment of my duties as Ambassador of the U.S.S.R. in your country I think it necessary first of all to underline that the Government and peoples of the Soviet Union, strangers to any aggressive intentions, wish to live in peace and good understanding with Great Britain, as well as with all parts of the British Empire. The policy of the U.S.S.R. is a policy of peace. This has been frequently illustrated in the past, and it finds extremely vivid expression at the present time.'

After quoting, as evidence of the latter assertion, the list of non-aggression treaties concluded, or on the way to conclusion, between the U.S.S.R. and other countries, and also the position of the Soviet delegation at the Disarmament Conference which had opened at Geneva in February, 1932, I continued:

'With all the greater readiness does the U.S.S.R. strive to develop friendly relations with Great Britain, with which it has such a variety of contacts in the economic sphere. The successful fulfilment of the first Five Year Plan, which has led to an immense growth in the productive forces of the U.S.S.R., and the forth-coming realization of the second Five Year Plan, the result of which will be a substantial rise in the prosperity of the working masses of our country, represent a good foundation for the development and strengthening of Soviet-British economic—and consequently political—relations.

'I hope that the common sense so characteristic of the British people, and their unsurpassed ability to reckon with facts (and the fifteen years' existence and development of the U.S.S.R. are an indisputable fact which cannot be avoided), will greatly facilitate the fulfilment of this task. Being of the greatest benefit to the two countries, the improvement of relations between them would at the same time represent an exceptionally powerful factor for international peace, which would be particularly important in our disturbing and difficult times.'

I concluded the statement with some words of a personal character:

'Personally, I received my appointment as Ambassador of the U.S.S.R. in Great Britain with great satisfaction. During the last twenty years I more than once have had to live and work in your country, and had the occasion to become better acquainted with the British people and British culture. I also have a feeling of gratitude to Britain which, in the years before the revolution, granted me the right of asylum as a political exile.[1] I should therefore feel particularly happy if I succeeded in promoting the cause of a *rapprochement* between the U.S.S.R. and Great Britain.'

The spirit with which the statement I had prepared was imbued is sufficiently clear not to require any comment.

Both my conversations with M. M. Litvinov took place in the first half of October, 1932. But on October 17 a telegram arrived from our Embassy in London, informing us that Sir John Simon, the British Foreign Secretary, had in a special Note, the day

1. The five years (1912–17) spent by me as an emigrant in London are described in my book of reminiscences, *Journey into the Past* (Hutchinson, 1962).

before, denounced the Anglo-Soviet Trade Agreement of 1930
which we had concluded with the second Labour Government.
This was an unexpected and obviously anti-Soviet act, on which
I shall have to dwell in greater detail. Two days later Litvinov
called me in and said:

'You were intending to begin your work in England with the
interview of which I approved the text. . . . Of course this would
have been a proper statement if normal relations existed between
the U.S.S.R. and Great Britain. But now, after the unilateral
denunciation of the Anglo-Soviet Trade Agreement, the situation
has changed. London has given an open demonstration of its
hostile disposition towards us. In such circumstances it is better
to refrain from an interview of such a friendly nature as yours.'

As a result, the interview quoted above died without being
born. I have included its text, however, in order to give a practical
illustration of the feelings which prevailed in Moscow when I was
taking my place in the train on the way to my work as Soviet
Ambassador in Great Britain.

I repeat with full conviction that the Soviet Government and
the Soviet people sincerely and seriously desired the establishment
of the best possible relations between the Soviet Union and Great
Britain.

But, as everyone knows, friendship is a bilateral act. It was not
enough for the Soviet side to desire the best possible relations
with Great Britain: the same desire was needed on the British
side too. Did it exist?

Let facts reply to this question.

2

What I found in England

I HAVE vivid recollections of the way the rulers of Britain met me in that distant autumn of 1932. It was a question, of course, not of myself as a person but of the Ambassador of the Soviet Union—and consequently of the Soviet Union as a people and a State. These recollections will show better than any long disquisitions the reply of the ruling classes of Britain to that entirely sincere desire for friendship and co-operation with which the Soviet Government and the Soviet people were animated.

The first recollection is in the sphere of Anglo-Soviet trade. I have already said that, when I was preparing for my journey, I intended in my ambassadorial activity to lay special emphasis on the expansion in every possible way of commercial operations between the two countries. Chance gave me an object-lesson of the difficulties I should have to meet on that very path.

On the eve of my arrival the *Sunday Chronicle* suddenly 'discovered' a terrifying event: Moscow, it appeared, had smuggled into Britain, 'in coffins of foreign origin', boxes of Russian matches on which the label depicted 'the Sacred Heart, transfixed by a dagger'! The newspaper raged in fury, and demanded that the Government should take most resolute steps against this kind of 'blasphemy'. The sensational story was immediately taken up by a number of other newspapers. An anti-Soviet wave rapidly rose in political and parliamentary circles. A furious campaign began against trade with the U.S.S.R. The atmosphere grew more hostile day by day. In vain did the director of Arcos[1] protest against these stupid charges, and insist that no anti-religious emblems were ever carried on Soviet matches: they would not listen to him. I do not know where all this outcry would have ended had it not happily been soon discovered that the notorious match-boxes had been delivered not from the Soviet Union but from India: and not in any 'coffins' but in the most prosaic wooden cases: and that the Indian manufacturers were least of all intending any blasphemy, since as Indians understand it a heart pierced by a dagger is a lofty and inspiring symbol.

Another recollection, of a somewhat different character. On November 8, 1932, I presented my credentials to the King, and consequently my position as Ambassador of the U.S.S.R. in Great Britain was legally established. The following day, November 9, I had to be present as Soviet representative at the Lord Mayor's annual banquet on the occasion of his entry upon his duties. This banquet is an extremely vivid ceremony in the medieval style, at which five or six hundred people are present, representing the genuine 'cream' of capitalist Britain. How rich this cream is can be judged even by the fact that of the Diplomatic Corps only Ambassadors are invited to the Lord Mayor's banquet: Ministers are not granted such an honour. The Lord Mayor's banquet is also an important political event. Tradition determines that the Prime Minister or some other prominent Cabinet Minister should make a big speech, in which he discusses some important and topical political question. It was at such a banquet that I found myself on November 9, 1932—and this is what happened (I quote the record I made the same day while it was fresh in my memory):

'The ceremony of presentation of guests as they arrive amounts to the following. At the far end of the long hall there stand on a small dais the newly elected Lord Mayor and his wife. From the entrance to the dais is spread a broad dark-red carpet,

1. Arcos—the All-Russian Co-operative Society—was at that time the central Soviet trading organization in Britain, legally established as a British commercial company.

along which each freshly arriving guest solemnly marches. A herald in Tudor costume pronounces his name for all to hear. The guest slowly walks to the end of the carpet, steps up on to the dais and shakes hands with the Lord Mayor and his wife. While the guest is advancing there is a thunder of applause in his honour from the guests already present. The amount of applause varies according to the position and popularity of the guest. The result is a peculiar kind of plebiscite, and from the volume of applause which is given to each guest one can judge infallibly the attitude of ruling quarters in Britain towards him.

'By chance it happened that I had to proceed along the red carpet immediately after the Japanese Ambassador, Matsudaira. It was a real ovation: he was applauded noisily, long and with enthusiasm. It was clear that his country and he himself were very popular among top people in Britain—and this in spite of the 'Manchurian incident'![1] Then the herald proclaimed:

' "His Excellency the Soviet Ambassador, Ivan Maisky!"

'It was as though an icy blast had swept through the hall. Everything at once fell silent. I moved off along the red carpet. Not a sound, not a handclap! A deadly, vigilantly hostile silence all round me. The brilliant assembly, crowded on either side of the carpet, accompanied me with curious and prickly glances. Beautifully attired dames pointed at me with their lorgnettes, whispering maliciously and even laughing. In this atmosphere of deafening hush I slowly, with head raised high, walked up the carpet and, as ritual dictated, shook hands with the Lord Mayor and his wife.'

It was a vivid and perfect demonstration of the sentiments of those who ruled Britain towards the Soviet Union.

And here is another episode. About a fortnight after the Lord Mayor's banquet there took place the opening of the new session of Parliament. This is also a very magnificent and colourful ceremony, in which the voice of the centuries can be heard.

1. That is what British ruling circles called Japan's seizure of north-eastern China, carried out in 1931.

The opening of Parliament takes place in the House of Lords. The peers are present in their red mantles trimmed with ermine, their wives in brilliant toilettes with their jewels, the notables of the State and the Diplomatic Corps. The King and Queen sit on a dais at the far end. Members of the House of Commons, by ancient tradition, are not allowed in the hall. A small group of their representatives stand (yes, stand and do not sit!) behind a special barrier which closes the exit from the House of Lords. The Lord Chamberlain with a deep bow hands the King the text of the Speech from the Throne. The King rises and reads it. Then the King and Queen, after bowing to all present, retire—and the session of Parliament is considered open.

My wife and I were at the opening of the new session of Parliament for 1932–3—a session which was fated to become so dramatic in the history of Anglo-Soviet relations (which I shall deal with later). As etiquette required, I sat with the other Ambassadors to the right of the throne, and my wife with the wives of other Ambassadors to the left. Etiquette also requires that the most honourable place be given to the wives of the Ambassadors, and only after them come the Court ladies of the highest rank. My wife at that time was the most junior of the Ambassadors' wives,[1] and therefore it turned out that by her side sat a senior female representative of the British aristocracy. She was a Duchess, as old as Methuselah and as ugly as a deadly sin, but all glittering in silks and diamonds. Before the ceremony opened, the Duchess began a conversation with my wife and, realizing that she was a foreigner, asked: 'And what country do you represent?'

My wife calmly answered: 'I represent the Soviet Union.'

---

1. Seniority in the Diplomatic Corps is determined by the period of presence of the Ambassador in the country where he is accredited. In the autumn of 1932 I was the last but one in the rank of Ambassadors in Britain, having only just arrived in London. The last was the German Ambassador, von Hoesch, who had presented his credentials to the King on the same day as myself, but a quarter of an hour after me. However, Hoesch was a bachelor, and therefore my wife was the most junior Ambassadress.

The effect of these words was shattering. The Duchess suddenly changed countenance as though she had stepped on a poisonous snake. She coloured frightfully, veins swelled on her scraggy neck, angry little lights glittered in her eyes. She brusquely drew away from my wife and cried out angrily: 'Do you know, I hate the Soviets!'

What had happened to British self-control, the most ordinary social politeness!

My wife did not lose her head, and in her turn sharply replied: 'In that event I am very sorry that you have proved to be my neighbour.'[1]

This little but so characteristic incident was an excellent supplement to what had happened at the Lord Mayor's banquet.

And finally one other recollection of the first weeks of my work in London as Soviet Ambassador.

Among the official visits which I paid after presenting my credentials was one to the then Chancellor of the Exchequer and *de facto* leader of the Conservative Party, Neville Chamberlain. During our talk Chamberlain began to complain that the U.S.S.R. was selling a great deal in Britain but buying little, and was spending what it realized in London on big orders placed in Germany. It was obvious that the Chancellor's heart was aching and crying to heaven at such 'injustice'. I answered tranquilly:

'Why are you surprised, Mr. Minister? The Soviet Government behaves as any good merchant would behave: it sells where it is more profitable and buys where it is more profitable.'

'But why do you consider that it is more profitable to place your orders in Germany and not in Britain?' asked Chamberlain.

1. This incident had the following diplomatic sequel. Two days after the incident I visited Mr. Monck, the head of the Protocol Department of the Foreign Office, told him what had happened at the opening of Parliament and asked him to take steps to see that in future my wife never had to sit by the side of the Duchess. Monck expressed his regret at the Duchess's lack of self-control, saying that she was the real *enfant terrible* at the British Court; and to do him justice he made sure that at various diplomatic lunches and dinners my wife and the Duchess were never again neighbours.

'For a very simple reason,' I replied. 'The Germans are giving us up to five years' credit, while you aren't.'

I had scarcely pronounced these words when Chamberlain's face took on an icy expression, he turned sharply in his chair and said with a kind of sinister deliberateness in his voice:

'Why, do you expect that we should give long-term credits to our enemies? No, we have better uses for our money.'

The real Chamberlain was in these words, genuine and without any make-up.

I replied in Chamberlain's own tones:

'I want absolutely nothing, Mr. Chamberlain. I haven't come to you for credits at all. . . . You asked me why the Soviet Union prefers to place its orders in Germany. I explained the reason to you, and that is all. The rest is your affair.'

What conclusion could I draw from these first and fleeting contacts with the rulers of Britain at that time? The conclusion could only be that they not only were not striving to establish friendly relations and co-operation with the land of the Soviets but on the contrary were openly displaying their hostility to it, occasionally even forgetting the most elementary rules of politeness and diplomatic tact.

3

The struggle for the Trade Agreement

THE next and more profound contacts with the British ruling class deepened such feelings in me still more.

My first large-scale diplomatic operation in London was negotiating a new trade agreement to replace the Agreement of 1930, which had been denounced by the Conservative Government. I do not hesitate to call the Government in power in 1932 Conservative, in spite of the fact that officially it was called 'National' and included, in addition to the Conservatives, the National Liberals headed by Simon and National Labour headed by MacDonald. I do this without hesitation, because of 520 M.P.s constituting the ruling coalition, 471 were Conservatives. Formally, the Prime Minister was Ramsay MacDonald, but the real Prime Minister was his deputy, Stanley Baldwin.

The negotiations for a new trade agreement which our then Trade Representative in Britain, A. V. Ozersky, a wise and skilful man, and I had to carry on in London proved to be extremely difficult, and lasted a full fifteen months. Why? Was it because the subject of negotiation was itself too complex? Was it because the contradictions in the commercial sphere between the U.S.S.R. and Great Britain were extremely acute? No, those were not the reasons. The negotiations proved difficult and protracted because the British Government constantly sought to apply to the Soviet Union a policy of hostile discrimination. This was the essence; and it was from this that all the main arguments and disputes sprang, sometimes assuming even a dramatic character.

For what was the course of events? I do not intend to set this forth in detail (I have done so in another book[1]), but I should recall here, briefly, the main points in the negotiations.

The Soviet Government understood perfectly that after the Imperial Conference at Ottawa, in the autumn of 1932, and the abandonment by Britain of free trade in favour of protection, a revision of the previous trade agreements between Great Britain and other countries was inevitable. Such a revision was in fact carried out step by step. But how was this usually done? Usually the British Government, without denouncing the old agreement, invited the Government concerned to enter upon negotiations in order to make in the agreement those changes which had become necessary owing to the radical alteration in British commercial policy. Such a method was entirely reasonable and legitimate, since it reduced to a minimum the difficulties which were involved in adapting British trade with the country concerned to the new conditions.

But how did the British Government act in relation to the U.S.S.R.? Quite differently.

On October 16, 1932, Sir John Simon, the Foreign Secretary, quite unexpectedly sent the Soviet Embassy in London a not very polite Note in which he stated that the British Government by unilateral act was denouncing the Anglo-Soviet Trade Agreement of 1930. For us this was a thunder-clap from a clear sky. The Soviet Government was confronted with a *fait accompli*, and one of a very unfriendly character. This character was emphasized still more by the fact that in his Note Simon did not even invite us to open negotiations for the completion of a new trade agreement, but only expressed his readiness 'to enter into discussion of the situation created by the denunciation' of the previous agreement.

Here was patent discrimination in respect of the U.S.S.R., discrimination No. 1.

Furthermore, what were the demands which the British Government put forward when trade negotiations did at last begin? They amounted in substance to two points:

1. The levelling-out of the balance of trade between the

1. *Recollections of a Soviet Ambassador in Britain* (Moscow, 1960).

U.S.S.R. and Great Britain, which till then had had an adverse balance of trade with us. But Britain also had an extremely adverse balance in her trade with the U.S.A., Germany, Argentine, Denmark and a number of other countries, yet had never required of them that this situation should be changed. The exception was now being made only for the U.S.S.R. This was discrimination No. 2.

2. The right of the British Government at any moment, by unilateral act, to restrict or even to prohibit the import of any Soviet goods into Britain if in its opinion such imports constituted a threat to Canada in the British market. The British Government had never put forward such claims to any other country. Only in respect of the U.S.S.R., once again, was there an exception. This was discrimination No. 3.

Not content with the two demands just mentioned, the British Government complicated the negotiations extremely by dragging in quite extraneous questions.

At that time, owing to the difficulties of the first Five Year Plan, there was a widespread conviction in the capitalist world that the attempt to industrialize the U.S.S.R. had failed, that the ground was shaky under the feet of the Soviet Government and that in the very near future the final collapse of the whole Soviet system could be expected. The strengthening of such views in Britain was assisted to no little degree by Sir Esmond Ovey, then British Ambassador in Moscow, who in the winter of 1932–3 sent dispatch upon dispatch to London on the internal situation of the U.S.S.R., each one gloomier than the last. The British Government, in particular Foreign Secretary Simon, willingly swallowed the information sent by Ovey (after all, they hoped so much that it was true!) and decided to take advantage of what seemed to them a favourable situation to settle their accounts with Moscow.

As a result, the London politicians set themselves the task of 'selling' the new trade agreement to the U.S.S.R. as dearly as possible. Therefore, in addition to satisfaction of the two demands mentioned above, they put forward as a condition for signing a new agreement that the U.S.S.R. should concede the following three points: compensation for the British capitalists who had lost by the October revolution, compensation for the 'losses' of the Anglo-American 'Lena Goldfields' company,[1] and finally (this may seem fantasy, but unfortunately it was a diplomatic reality) that prices for goods sold in the *Torgsin* shops should correspond to prices on the world market.[2]

1. 'Lena Goldfields' had received a concession for working the gold deposits on the Lena from the Tsarist Government in 1908. The October revolution put an end to this concession; but in 1925, on the basis of the Concessions Decree of the Soviet Government of 1920, the company concluded a new concession agreement (of course, on different conditions from those of the past) and developed gold production on a large scale. In 1929 about 15,000 people were working in its employment. As, however, Lena Goldfields, which had now been transformed from a British into an Anglo-American concern, was systematically trying to carry on its business on capitalist lines, and was constantly infringing Soviet law, there were friction and disputes all the time between the company and the Soviet Government. In 1930, in keeping with the concession agreement, it was decided to settle all the disputed questions by arbitration, and the personal composition of the court of arbitration was even agreed between the two sides. But one week before the date appointed for hearing the case Lena Goldfields carried out a lock-out, and even closed its office in Moscow. These actions by the company patently infringed the concessions agreement. Juridically, as well as in effect, the agreement ceased to exist, and the Soviet Government, naturally, found it impossible to take part in arbitration provided under a concession agreement which had lost its validity. None the less, Lena Goldfields insisted on the two remaining members of the court (the President and the representative of the company) examining the dispute, even though the Soviet representative was absent. This pseudo-arbitration produced the verdict that the Soviet Government should pay the company £3,500,000 for the capital invested by the company and another £9,500,000 as compensation for the profits which the company had reckoned to receive during the twenty-five years remaining before the agreement expired. Naturally, the Soviet Government decisively rejected these entirely groundless claims. And now, at the beginning of 1933, the British Government (and particularly Sir John Simon) made an attempt to procure for the company its pound of flesh as part of the negotiations for the conclusion of a new Anglo-Soviet trade agreement.

2. At the end of 1932 there were set up in the U.S.S.R. *Torgsin* shops (this was an abbreviation for *Torgovlya s inostrantsami*—'trade with foreigners'), which were particularly well supplied with foodstuffs and

Such was the degree of unceremoniousness reached by the British Government at the time! This was discrimination No. 4.

Quite obviously the attitude adopted by the British side in the trade negotiations itself made an agreement extremely difficult to reach. But the situation grew still worse when, in March, 1933, a new and exceptionally explosive factor came into play.

During the first Five Year Plan the Soviet Government had technical aid agreements with a number of large firms in the capitalist countries. Among these firms was the well-known British concern, Metropolitan-Vickers. It maintained a special office in Moscow, and its engineers were engaged on various Soviet building sites. On March 12, 1933, about twenty-five employees of Metropolitan-Vickers in the U.S.S.R., including six British engineers, were arrested on charges of espionage and wrecking.

This event aroused a violent reaction in Britain, and the Government itself supported and magnified it in every possible way. Once again an extremely sinister role in this was played by

---

consumer goods, and in which goods were sold in exchange for gold, valuables and foreign currency. The purpose of *Torgsin* was to concentrate in the hands of the Government the gold and other valuables in the possession of the population, and thereby enlarge the resources of the State required to pay for imported machinery and equipment. At the same time there were closed down the *Insnab* shops, where foreign diplomats in Moscow bought foodstuffs and other commodities in unlimited quantity for Soviet currency (in those years there was rationing for foodstuffs and other goods sold to the people). In practice the system of supplying the foreign diplomats through *Insnab* led to numerous abuses on their part, and served as a means of illicit enrichment of many of them. With the opening of the *Torgsin* shops, foreign diplomats were invited henceforth to satisfy their requirements of foodstuffs and other goods there, i.e. to pay for the commodities they required in gold or in foreign currency. This deprived the diplomatic speculators of a considerable income, and many of them made noisy protest against the measures taken by the Soviet Government. At the head of the discontented diplomats stood Sir Esmond Ovey, British Ambassador in Moscow. This was why the British side in the trade negotiations presented such a stupid and offensive demand to the Soviet Government.

the British Ambassador in Moscow. If, immediately after the
arrest of the British engineers, Ovey had confined himself to
enquiring the reasons for the arrest, and also to making sure that
the arrested men were held in good conditions, that the investigation should proceed without delay and that the accused should be
assured of a proper defence, no one could have objected to his
actions. The direct obligation of any Ambassador is to show
interest in and concern for his fellow citizens who have been
subjected to repressive action in the country where he is accredited. But Ovey went much further. Brought up in British Great
Power traditions, he imagined that he could dictate his conditions
to the Soviet State. This was discrimination No. 5.

In fact, on the afternoon of March 12, a few hours after the
arrest and before the investigation had even begun, Ovey assured
Simon that the British engineers were absolutely innocent, and
recommended the British Government to demand their immediate liberation without investigation and without trial. The
British Government accepted the recommendation of its Ambassador and began furious pressure on the Soviet Government,
insisting that the prosecution of the six British subjects should be
stopped. Should we refuse, Ovey threatened that there would be
a rupture of Anglo-Soviet relations. M. M. Litvinov in Moscow
and I in London had vigorously to repel these claims as an
intolerable interference in our internal affairs. The British
were firmly told that the engineers would come before a Soviet
court, whatever the reaction of the British Government might
be.

Then the politicians in London decided to take more drastic
measures. Lulled by Ovey's misinformation about the internal
situation in the U.S.S.R., and also by his reports, subjectively
retouched, on his conversations with Litvinov about the
Metropolitan-Vickers case, they calculated that they would
secure, at the least, the immediate liberation of the British
engineers, and at the most they might even assist the Soviet
Government to descend into its grave a little more rapidly.

The London politicians began by demonstratively breaking off the trade negotiations on March 20. As we met this step with complete calm, they went on to other measures of a repressive character, on the details of which I do not need to dwell. It will be sufficient to say that, in spite of all the efforts of the British Government, the trial did take place in Moscow, and that one of the British engineers was acquitted, three were expelled from the U.S.S.R. and two were sentenced to three and two years' imprisonment respectively. However, the politicians in London, once having entered on the path of blackmail, could not stop themselves and, moving along it at accelerating speed, brought matters to the point of a three months' trade war between Britain and the U.S.S.R. The British Government imposed a ban on Soviet imports into Great Britain, in reply to which the Soviet Government imposed a ban on British imports into the U.S.S.R. This trade war ended only on July 1, 1933, by a mutual lifting of the bans on each other's goods, and also by the pardoning and expulsion from the U.S.S.R. of the two British engineers sentenced to imprisonment. On July 3 trade negotiations also were resumed.

There were very many difficulties in these negotiations—difficulties arising from the policy of discrimination towards the U.S.S.R. pursued by the British Government—and these difficulties did not disappear after the trade war had been ended. Nevertheless, combining firmness and flexibility in its tactics, the Soviet Government brought the negotiations to a successful conclusion. On February 16, 1934, the new Trade Agreement was signed. True, it bore the title of 'Temporary': but more than a quarter of a century has passed since that date and the 'Temporary' Agreement is still in force, still regulating the development of Anglo-Soviet trade.

What impression was left in my mind by the tactics of multi-stage discrimination used by the British Government in the course of the struggle for a trade agreement? What conclusion was I bound to make from the experience of my first serious diplomatic operation in London?

It did not diverge in any way from the impressions I had

C

formed immediately on my arrival in Britain. On the contrary, it only confirmed that they were correct. Now I could see still more clearly that the group ruling the country was full of hostility to the U.S.S.R., and made concessions to it only when circumstances beyond their control obliged them to do so. As a result, my feeling of distrust towards the rulers of Britain not only did not lessen but rather increased. I felt this most acutely in regard to a particular group of politicians of whom I shall yet have to speak later—a group whose outstanding representative was Simon.

Officially the negotiations on the British side were conducted by Simon as Foreign Secretary and Runciman as President of the Board of Trade. But Runciman did not take any effective part in the negotiations. During all these fifteen months he appeared only twice—at the first meeting, when the talks began, and at the last, when the Trade Agreement was being signed. In all other respects Runciman's presence was not felt at all, while the officials of his Ministry, who really carried on the negotiations, had for the most part a reasonable attitude. They sincerely wanted Anglo-Soviet trade to develop and, so far as the general directives of the British Government permitted, sought not to complicate but on the contrary to facilitate the conclusion of an agreement.

It was otherwise with Simon and his officials. In spite of his Liberal past, Simon in the thirties was one of the most implacable enemies of the Soviet Union. In the course of the negotiations he constantly strove not to shorten but to prolong the road to agreement. It was he who sought out every possible pretext for complicating the negotiations by various extraneous questions like the ludicrous one of the prices in the *Torgsin* shops. Simon's heart beat in unison with the interests of the most hardened representatives of the capitalist world like the Lena Goldfields company, and for their sake he was ready to sacrifice even the interests of British trade. In addition to all this Simon was a man who was not fastidious in his choice of means to achieve his ends, and made wide use of sheer invention in the struggle against the U.S.S.R. Apart from a few pleasant exceptions, the machinery of the British Foreign Office in those years was saturated with the Simon spirit.

I remember one example. The trade negotiations were approaching their very end. Everything had been agreed except the question of *Torgsin*. But Simon on this account was delaying the signature of the agreement. I then invited the well-known Liberal journalist A. J. Cummings, with whom at that time I had good relations, to come to see me, and I frankly told him why the business was still not concluded. Next day, February 2, 1934, the *News Chronicle* published on its front page, under a big heading 'The British Ambassador's Potatoes', a virulent article by Cummings explaining the true reason for the delay in signature. This article caused the utmost confusion in political quarters in London, and a Labour M.P., Grenfell, put down a question asking what was the connection between signature of the Trade Agreement and the food supplies of the British Ambassador in Moscow. Simon himself gave the official reply—and this is what he said:

'There is no truth in the suggestion that the Anglo-Soviet Trade Agreement is being held up because of this matter.'

So limitless was the extent to which Simon's falsehoods carried him. Can one be surprised that this only reinforced Soviet distrust of the ruling class of Great Britain?

4

A brief thaw and its causes

ABOUT the middle of 1934 a temporary—or more correctly a brief—thaw began in Anglo-Soviet relations. There were two main reasons for this.

The first was that in January, 1933, Hitler came to power in Germany. At first the rulers of Britain did not take the Fuehrer too seriously. I well remember how throughout 1933 British politicians of various hues—Conservatives, Liberals, Labour Party men—were still arguing about whether Hitler would succeed in holding on to power. Even such an experienced states-man as Vansittart, who then held the key post of Permanent Under-Secretary for Foreign Affairs, said to me in the course of a conversation in the summer of 1933:

'Hitler has many difficulties and enemies, external and internal, to contend with. . . . The French, the Belgians, the Czechs and the Poles are extremely suspicious of him. . . . Things are not too peaceful within the Nazi Party. . . . There are men who aspire to the first place in its ranks, and it will not be easy for Hitler to cope with them. . . . You cannot exclude the possibility that the internal struggle will break up the Nazi Party. . . . We must wait and see.'

As for the Labour Party leaders, most of them were convinced that Nazi domination in Germany would not be for long.

However, from 1934 onwards, and particularly from the middle of the year after Hitler had destroyed the Roehm group and in general had crushed the internal opposition in his party, the mood in British ruling circles began to change. They began to understand that Hitlerism was consolidating itself and would

36

have to be reckoned with seriously, at least for a number of years. This aroused anxiety and alarm among them. It brought back memories of the events and circumstances of the first world war, when Great Britain had the greatest difficulty in protecting her position in the world against the dangerous attacks of German imperialism. The aspirations, the watchwords, the demands of Hitler obviously foreshadowed the rebirth of the old plans of German hegemony which had played such a great part in letting loose the first world war—even, perhaps, in a still more menacing form than in those days. The ruling circles of Great Britain were faced more and more insistently with the question of what was to be done.

Their first reaction centred round the idea that the Entente of the first world war period should be restored: that is, a military alliance of Britain, France and Russia against Germany. True, in place of Tsarist Russia there was now the Union of Soviet Socialist Republics: this was unpleasant, very unpleasant, but in the long run international politics are guided not by emotions but by practical interests. If interests so require one must swallow even a bitter medicine. It so happened that at the time I am describing not only Labour and Liberal politicians began seriously to think of improving relations with the Soviet Union, but also many Conservatives.

The second reason for the beginning of the thaw was that, after the dispute over the Metropolitan-Vickers case, British ruling quarters became finally convinced of the strength and solidity of the U.S.S.R., and drew the conclusion that henceforth the 'Soviet factor' had become a permanent element in the world situation. Independently of one's sympathies or antipathies, it would have to be taken into account in all political calculations and projects. And as British politicians have always been distinguished by their ability to reckon with facts (even unpleasant ones), they began after the signature of the Trade Agreement in 1934 to consider how best to utilize in their own interests the power of the U.S.S.R., which had been displayed so unexpectedly. And their thoughts, as I have just said, began to turn more

and more to the traditional road of the Entente of the first world
war.

One chance circumstance greatly promoted such a change in
the state of mind of the ruling circles of Great Britain. Between
February and April, 1934, there took place the memorable 'epic
of the *Chelyuskin*'. About one hundred Soviet people, including
women and children, with Otto Yulievich Schmidt at their head,
after the sinking of the *Chelyuskin* found themselves on a Polar
icefloe far from the land. The western world, its press, its
politicians, its scientists, its Arctic explorers, considered that the
'Chelyuskinites' were lost, and intoned their funeral dirge. But
the Soviet world thought and felt otherwise. The 'Chelyuskinites'
not only did not fall into panic or lose heart, but created on the
icefloe an amazing organized collective, which held high the
banner of the Soviet Union, carried on its scientific work, looked
after the health and maintained the high spirits of its members.
O. Y. Schmidt, as head of the icefloe camp, even gave his com-
rades a course of lectures on historical materialism. At the same
time the Soviet Government and the Soviet people mobilized all
that was possible to save their fellow countrymen from disaster.
Men, resources, technique, the radio, aircraft—everything was
concentrated to serve this noble purpose, and finally all the
'Chelyuskinites' were saved, including the eight dogs in the
camp, who were brought out on planes with the rest.

Polar dramas have always engaged the sympathetic attention
of the great mass of mankind. The *Chelyuskin* drama won that
concern with particular force both because its victims included
a hundred men, women and children and because the existence of
wireless made it possible to follow every event, even the tiniest,
in the life of the camp on the ice. The courageous behaviour of
the 'Chelyuskinites' aroused universal admiration in all circles,
irrespective of political views and inclinations. At the same
time the colossal energy and the vast expenditure of the Soviet
State employed in saving the 'Chelyuskinites' amazed the
bourgeois world. I remember Lloyd George saying to me in
those days:

'It's stupendous! No other Government would have made such efforts to save Arctic explorers. . . . It's very noble . . . and very wise!'

There was a sly gleam in the eyes of the Liberal leader as he suddenly and unexpectedly added: 'I congratulate you! You have won a great diplomatic victory.'

Lloyd George was right. This 'epic of the *Chelyuskin*' had not only once more confirmed the strength and vitality of the Soviet State but had also vividly displayed—and displayed to the whole wide world—its nobility, its humanity, its profound wisdom. At one stroke the popularity of the U.S.S.R. rose higher, particularly among the working people in all quarters of the globe, than years and years of stubborn propaganda work could have raised it. An external expression of this was the fact that for many months the portrait of O. Y. Schmidt was constantly appearing in the capitalist press.

The 'epic of the *Chelyuskin*' played no small part, therefore, in developing the thaw in Anglo-Soviet relations which began in the middle of 1934. Pyschologically it helped many who were unfriendly to the U.S.S.R. to change to new political attitudes.

As a result of all these circumstances, those elements who favoured a rebirth of the Entente temporarily gained the upper hand among British ruling circles.

Here it will be timely to say that in the period between the two world wars the British ruling class split into two main groups on the question of relations with the U.S.S.R.

In one the principle of State interest prevailed. This group saw that Britain and the U.S.S.R. as Powers have no serious contradictions, while in the economic sphere they may even be very useful to each other. This group supported the policy of a *rapprochement* with the U.S.S.R. Its most prominent representatives were people like Lloyd George, Beaverbrook, Eden, Vansittart and others. After Hitler had come to power Churchill also joined this group.

In the other group, on the contrary, the predominant feeling was blind class hatred of the U.S.S.R. as a country of Socialism. This group considered it essential in all circumstances to attack the Soviet Union, even to the detriment of the national interests of Britain as a State. Its most prominent representatives were Lord Curzon, the brothers Chamberlain (Austen and Neville), Lord Birkenhead, Joynson-Hicks, Simon, Halifax and others. Up to 1934 Churchill also was with this group.

What was the comparative strength of the two groups? It was not of course constant, but changed from year to year in keeping with various events and circumstances. Yet as a whole the 'class hatred group' (which I shall call for convenience the 'Chamberlainites') was much more influential than the 'State interest group' (which I shall call 'Churchillites'). In the middle and the second half of the thirties the distribution of forces within the ruling class of Great Britain, taking the Conservatives and the Liberals together, was roughly as follows: three-quarters of the Conservatives followed Chamberlain and only about one-quarter adopted Churchill's attitude, while the Liberals were divided roughly equally between the two groups, but were already dramatically declining and had lost the greater part of their former political influence. It is clear, consequently, that in the period I have in mind the Chamberlainites played the decisive part in the ranks of the ruling class, particularly bearing in mind that in the period between the two world wars they were too long in power, and had been able to fill the greater part of the State machine with their supporters.

Of course, the Chamberlainites had to reckon with the Labour Party, which by the middle thirties had already become the second main party in Britain, displacing the Liberals.[1] The

1. The outcome of the Parliamentary elections in November, 1935, will give some idea of the relationship of forces between the various parties at that time:

Party	No. of votes (thousands)	No. of seats
Conservatives	10,489	387
National Liberals (Simon Group) . . .	867	33

British working class undoubtedly wanted to maintain the most friendly relations with the Soviet State, and had shown this most vividly in 1920 by thwarting the attempt to engage Britain in military intervention against Soviet Russia during the Soviet-Polish war. But in its practical activity the Labour Party far from fully reflected these feelings of the masses. Worst of all in this respect was the top leadership. Up to 1931 Ramsay MacDonald, Philip Snowden, J. H. Thomas and several others almost openly strove to turn the policy of their party in an anti-Soviet direction. After they had been expelled in 1931 and, on forming the ephemeral National Labour Party, had deserted to the Conservative camp, there could always be felt among the orthodox members remaining in the Labour Party a definite current of opinion which secretly sympathized with the expelled leaders, but avoided speaking of this openly.

As a result, the resistance of the Labour Opposition to the Chamberlainites turned out to be much weaker than could have been the case. This in turn opened to the Chamberlainites a sufficiently broad field of activity for sabotaging any Anglo-Soviet *rapprochement*.

National Labour (Macdonald Group) . .	340	8
Others	97	3
Government Coalition (total)	11,793	431
Labour	8,465	158
Opposition Liberals	1,382	21
Communists	27	1
Others	275	4
Opposition (total)	10,149	184

These figures show beyond doubt that by the middle thirties the Conservative and Labour parties were the two main parties in the country, that the Liberals now had fallen back to third place, and that MacDonald's 'National Labour' Party was almost a figure of speech. This meant that three-quarters of the Conservatives plus half the Liberals, given a certain passivity of the Labour leadership, were able effectively to sabotage an Anglo-Soviet *rapprochement*.

However that might be, the existence of these two groups in the ranks of the ruling class and the constant struggle between them were a standing feature of the whole history of Anglo-Soviet relations between the two world wars. Now this, now that grouping, with the Labour Opposition as a make-weight, left its impression on the practical steps taken by the British Government in relation to the U.S.S.R. From the middle of 1934, for reasons I have explained earlier, the Churchillites temporarily gained the upper hand, and this found its expression in a number of hard facts.

5

Steps to a *rapprochement*

CHRONOLOGICALLY, the first of such facts was a series of lengthy conversations between Vansittart and myself, as Soviet Ambassador, in July–August, 1934. The conversations began on the initiative of Vansittart, and the form which he gave to this initiative was a very curious one.

On June 21, 1934, my wife and I were invited to lunch with the Vansittarts. There were ten people present, among them Sir John Simon. However, the lunch was arranged in honour of myself and my wife, not of Simon. This was clear from the fact that, as British etiquette required, I was seated to the right of the hostess and my wife to the right of the host, while Simon was seated to the left of the hostess, and consequently was No. 2. During the luncheon, when there was a crossfire of conversations over the table, Lady Vansittart leaned slightly in my direction and asked: 'Well, how do you like life in London?'

Something in her tone and in the expression on her face gave me to understand that her question was not simply customary society small-talk. However, I cautiously replied: 'London is a fine city, but I meet with great difficulties here.'

Lady Vansittart bent still closer and asked in a half-whisper: 'I suppose it's my neighbour on the left who is making these difficulties?'

She had Simon in mind, of course. I nodded.

'Then why should you not have a frank talk about this with Van?' Lady Vansittart gave this familiar title to her husband.

I knew that Simon and Vansittart did not get on politically, since they were representatives of two different diplomatic lines

43

of policy: still, I had not expected that Lady Vansittart would give me so frankly to understand that there were differences between the Foreign Secretary and his Permanent Under-Secretary.

'In the atmosphere created around the Soviet Embassy in London,' I replied, 'it seemed to me inconvenient to display any initiative in this respect.'

'Oh, is that so?' exclaimed Lady Vansittart. 'If it's only a question of who speaks first, that difficulty is easily overcome. . . . I will undertake it myself.'

It was clear to me that on the lips of Lady Vansittart were the words of the Permanent Under-Secretary himself. However, I could not rid myself of a certain dose of scepticism. Women are emotional beings, and I was afraid that in her conversation this elegant little woman might have gone further than the 'instructions' which she had received from her husband.

But I was mistaken. Lady Vansittart's mediation had a practical result. Two days later Vansittart rang me up and invited me to come to the Foreign Office to talk about Anglo-Soviet relations. On July 3 I had my first long talk with Vansittart, and on July 12 and 18 two more. All of them were of a very frank nature, and were characterized by a highly constructive spirit. We examined all the questions then outstanding between the U.S.S.R. and Great Britain and came to the conclusion that, although there were in some cases differences of opinion between the two governments, they could not be an obstacle to a serious improvement of relations between them.

A particularly important part in our conversations was played by the question of the so-called Eastern Locarno. At that time, with a view to strengthening European security, the French Minister for Foreign Affairs, M. Barthou, was carrying on energetic propaganda for a draft pact of mutual assistance between the U.S.S.R., Poland, Latvia, Estonia, Lithuania, Finland and Czechoslovakia. France was to be a guarantor for the Eastern Locarno, while the U.S.S.R. was to become a guarantor for the existing Western Locarno. The U.S.S.R. sympathized with Barthou's plan. Britain's position was unclear.

In my first conversation with Vansittart I strove to convince him of the necessity for Britain to support Barthou's draft. On July 8 Barthou himself came to London and had talks on the same subject with the British Government. During our second conversation, on July 12, Vansittart told me that Britain would declare in favour of an Eastern Locarno if Germany were admitted to it. The Soviet Union and France accepted this condition, and thereupon the London Government announced its support for an Eastern Locarno. However, Germany, followed by Poland, refused to enter the proposed group. This dealt a mortal blow to the whole scheme. But in my conversations with Vansittart the affair of the Eastern Locarno played a very positive part, and the Soviet Government's agreement that Germany should be included convinced him of the sincerity of the Soviet Union's striving for peace.

Litvinov was very satisfied with my conversations with Vansittart, seeing in them the first steps in the reduction of tension in Anglo-Soviet relations. In fact, as later events showed, this frank exchange of opinions in London opened the way for the British Government's support for entry of the U.S.S.R. into the League of Nations, which I will speak of later.

Here I want to say a few words about Vansittart. A clever and cultivated man, a skilful diplomat and politician, a talented poet and writer, he was, of course, flesh of the flesh of the ruling class of Great Britain. His divinity was the British Empire. The maintenance of its integrity and inviolability, the defence of the world position of British imperialism, were Vansittart's symbol of faith. Taking this as his point of departure, he manœuvred now to the right and now to the left, in particular changing his attitude to the U.S.S.R.

It is well known that after the second world war Vansittart, like many other British statesmen, became an antagonist of our country. The reason was that the war did not end as the leaders of the ruling class of Great Britain had wished. They had anticipated that the U.S.S.R. would emerge from the war much enfeebled, that for a long time it would not be able to carry on any active

foreign policy, and that for at least a whole generation, if not
more, it would cease to disturb the sleep of the London politicians. When in reality things turned out quite otherwise, when it
transpired that the U.S.S.R. was much stronger after the war
than before it, and that in addition there had come into being
around it a powerful Socialist camp, it was not only the
Chamberlainites, but the Churchillites too, beginning with
Churchill himself, who bristled up against the U.S.S.R. It was
strange for me to read some of Vansittart's post-war pronouncements against our country, so shallow and hackneyed were they.
What had happened to his intelligence, his education, his subtle
play of thought, his literary art? That is what it means to go
against the forces of historical progress, against mankind's
tomorrow!

However, then, in the middle of the thirties, immediately after
the consolidation of Hitlerism in Germany, Vansittart was a
warm supporter of the rebirth of the Entente, and took advantage
of his position in the British machinery of government really to
do a great deal in this direction. If the Entente nevertheless did
not come into being before the beginning of the second world
war, the blame for this in any case does not fall upon Vansittart.

The second factor in point of time which bore witness to the
beginning of a thaw in Anglo-Soviet relations was the affair of
the entry of the U.S.S.R. into the League of Nations. When the
League was formed in 1919, as is well known, Soviet Russia was
not invited to become a member. At that time, and for the next
fifteen years, the League of Nations was a hot-bed of hostility,
plots and intrigues of every kind against the Soviet State. By 1934
the world situation had changed considerably compared with
1919, and this found its reflection in the destinies of the League
of Nations. In 1920 the American Senate had rejected ratification
of the Versailles Treaty, as a result of which the U.S.A. had not
joined the League. In 1933 Japan and Germany, having taken the
path of active aggression, had withdrawn from the League. There
remained as the League's bosses Britain and France, who visibly
had not the power to steer the ship in the conditions, which

became increasingly clear, of an international thunderstorm. This forced the leaders of the Anglo-French bloc to turn their minds to the question of bringing the U.S.S.R. into the League. In its turn the Soviet Government, by the end of 1933, had come to the conclusion that in these conditions it would be useful for the U.S.S.R. to join the League of Nations. This would place at its disposal an international platform, most important at that time, from which to defend peace and counteract the peril of a second world war. It also opened up a possibility—though the Soviet Government never over-estimated its significance—of raising obstacles in the path of those who would launch a new world massacre. As a result, the U.S.S.R., in September, 1934, became a member of the League, with a permanent seat on its Council.

Of course, the way had to be well prepared. A great part in this was played by the then French Minister for Foreign Affairs. In the first years after the October Revolution M. Barthou had been one of the most determined enemies of Soviet Russia, and for all practical purposes it was he who had sabotaged the Genoa Conference of 1922. However, being a sincere (though Conservative) patriot, he later understood that with the coming of Hitlerism to power in Germany French security depended greatly on co-operation with the U.S.S.R. With much vigour he set about achieving this end. He was particularly active in campaigning for the entry of the Soviet Union into the League of Nations. He encountered many obstacles, but ultimately succeeded in overcoming them. In Britain his helper at this time was Vansittart. They worked together and in September, 1935, thirty States-members of the League of Nations approached the Soviet Government with the invitation to become a member. On behalf of the Soviet Government M. M. Litvinov most skilfully carried through all the preliminary conversations and arrangements for the entry of the U.S.S.R. When this had happened Vansittart said to me:

'Well, now we have become members of one and the same club. I hope that from now on our relations will be such as ought to prevail between members of the same club.'

These words of Vansittart were confirmed to some extent
at the next Lord Mayor's banquet on November 9, 1934, when I
had a very different reception. This time the library was not filled
with the deafening silence which had greeted me two years before.
Instead the notables applauded. They applauded in moderation,
without enthusiasm or fervour, but at any rate sufficiently loudly
to enable one to conclude that there had been a considerable
change in the state of mind of the top people in relation to the
U.S.S.R.

The third factor, speaking chronologically, which bore
evidence that a thaw had begun was the visit of Eden to Moscow
in March, 1935. It was Vansittart again who played a very
great part in preparing and carrying through this diplomatic
action.

Eden had then only begun to gain promotion. Coming from
the landed gentry of middle rank, a cultivated and educated man,
he possessed a considerable amount of common sense and reliable
political instinct. After Hitler came to power he began to consider
that the British Empire could be saved only by the rebirth of the
Entente, and therefore joined that grouping in the Conservative
Party which advocated a *rapprochement* between Britain and the
U.S.S.R. He even justified his attitude by quite serious historical
arguments. I remember how in 1943, while the war was raging,
when I was leaving London to take up my post as Deputy
People's Commissar for Foreign Affairs in Moscow, Eden in a
speech at a farewell luncheon said:

'During the last century and a half England and Russia have
always been in the same camp when any serious crisis arose in
Europe. That is what happened in the time of Napoleon, it was the
same in the years of the first world war and it has happened now
in the days of the second world war. What is the explanation? It is
that Britain and Russia are two great and powerful States at
opposite ends of Europe who cannot reconcile themselves to the
creation in Europe of the unquestioned domination of any third
power. Such an excessively powerful third State becomes a menace
both to Britain and to Russia—and as a result they unite against

it and ultimately bring about its downfall. The trouble only has been that, once the crisis was over, England and Russia hitherto have gone off in different directions and even begun to quarrel. This opened the way for the appearance of some new pretender to dominate Europe, or even the whole world. The greatest problem of modern diplomacy, both British and Soviet, is to avert the repetition of this process after the end of the present war.'

Unfortunately, Eden proved unable to maintain this attitude after the war, and gradually joined the ranks of the knights of the 'cold war' proclaimed by the leaders of America, and supported by the leaders of British imperialism.

But at that time, in the thirties, Eden energetically supported the policy of *rapprochement* with the U.S.S.R., and for practical purposes it was by this that he made his career. When I arrived in London at the end of 1932 Eden was Parliamentary Under-Secretary for Foreign Affairs in the House of Commons, and as Simon was also a member of that House and spoke there on all the more important questions of foreign policy, Eden had to play a secondary role. But later Eden's elevation proceeded at a rapid pace. This was partly due to his connections in the upper ranks of the Conservative Party; but of still greater significance was that struggle between the two groupings within the ruling circles of Great Britain which I mentioned earlier. The supporters of a 'rebirth of the Entente' saw in Eden a man suitable for their purpose, and began to promote him.

In 1934 Eden was appointed Lord Privy Seal (a purely decorative post), in fact a Minister without Portfolio, in Baldwin's Cabinet. He was given the special task of dealing with League of Nations affairs. As a result there were for a certain time in Britain two Foreign Secretaries—a 'senior', Simon, and a 'junior', Eden. They represented two different, and on a number of questions even opposite, lines of British foreign policy. The relations between them were strained. Vansittart, who also did not get on well with Simon, supported Eden. As a result there went on within the British Foreign Office a constant internal struggle, which only reflected the struggle going on over

D

questions of foreign policy among the ruling circles of the country as a whole.

At the beginning of 1935 there was to be a visit to Berlin by Simon and Eden, for talks with Hitler. Everything had been arranged, and the British Ministers were preparing to leave, when suddenly, in February, Hitler publicly tore up the military articles of the Versailles Treaty and proclaimed that henceforth Germany would arm without regard to any restrictions. This new 'leap' of the Nazi Fuehrer caused the greatest excitement in Britain and France. The British Ministers' visit to Berlin was left hanging in mid-air. An acute conflict began in British ruling circles between the supporters of an Entente and those who wanted appeasement of the aggressors. The supporters of an Entente argued that in the situation now created a visit of the British Ministers to Berlin would be the greatest humiliation for Britain, and would only whet the appetite of Hitler. The supporters of appeasement replied that, the more real the danger of aggression, the more necessary was it to make use of even the most insignificant ways and means of preserving peace. Finally they arrived at a compromise: Simon and Eden would go to Berlin, and from there Eden would continue on the way to Moscow, for talks with the Soviet Government.

That is how Eden's visit to the U.S.S.R. took place.

Today Moscow has become a centre of attraction for the Heads of States and Ministers of various nations from all ends of the earth. We have become accustomed to it, and treat it as a matter of course. At that time the situation was quite different. For eighteen years after the October Revolution Moscow had been taboo for leaders of the capitalist world. Moscow was under political boycott—not formally but in effect. No Minister of the large western States thought it possible to set foot on Moscow soil. And now suddenly, in March, 1935, Eden, a member of the Government of then still extremely powerful Great Britain, appeared in Moscow! This was an event of great political importance, and aroused much comment in the world press.

On the instructions of the Soviet Government, I accompanied

Eden on his journey from Berlin to Moscow. I was present at all
the conversations between Eden and the leaders of the U.S.S.R.,
sometimes serving as an interpreter. In particular, I attended the
meeting between J. V. Stalin and Eden, and accompanied the
latter on his visit to the sights of the Soviet capital. Eden, I
remember, was particularly interested in our collections of the
French painters (Gauguin, Cézanne, Renoir and others), a visit
to which he had included in his Moscow programme while still
in London. Eden also took a trip along the first line of the Moscow
Metro.

The three days' negotiations revealed a large identity of views
of the two sides on international questions. Litvinov instructed
me to draw up a draft communiqué, to be published at the very
end of the visit. I did this. Eden on his side appointed William
Strang, an official of the British Foreign Office dealing with
League of Nations affairs, who had earlier served as Counsellor
of the British Embassy in Moscow, to join in working out the
communiqué. We met at the British Embassy on Sofiiskaya
Embankment, and very rapidly arrived at an agreement: Strang
made only minor alterations of a textual character in the draft we
submitted. Then the communiqué prepared in this way was finally
approved by both sides, and appeared in the press on April 1,
1935. Its most important passage read as follows:

'The representatives of the two governments were happy to
note, as a result of a full and frank exchange of views, that there is
at present no conflict of interest between the two governments on
any of the main issues of international policy, and that this fact
provides a firm foundation for the development of fruitful
collaboration between them in the cause of peace.

'They are confident that both countries, recognizing that the
integrity and prosperity of each is to the advantage of the other,
will govern their mutual relations in that spirit of collaboration
and loyalty to obligations assumed by them which is inherent in
their common membership of the League of Nations.'

The Soviet side was satisfied with the visit and with the
communiqué, and Eden was too. In conversation with me he said

he was pleased with his visit to Moscow, and thought the communiqué very good.

The presence of a thaw was still further confirmed by two other events which immediately followed Eden's visit. On May 2, 1935, a Pact of Mutual Assistance was signed in Paris between France and the U.S.S.R., following which Pierre Laval, the French Minister for Foreign Affairs, paid a visit to the Soviet capital. On May 16, 1935, a Pact of Mutual Assistance was signed in Prague between the U.S.S.R. and Czechoslovakia, and soon after this the Czechoslovak Minister for Foreign Affairs, Eduard Benes, also visited the Soviet Union.

I need hardly say that personally I was extremely pleased with what had happened. I even began to admit the thought that a new page had been opened in Anglo-Soviet relations, a page of prolonged and systematic improvement. At all events I very much wanted this to happen. I was worried only by the thought that the negotiations in Moscow were conducted, and the communiqué was signed by Eden—a supporter of *rapprochement* with the U.S.S.R. Of course, he could not have done this without the agreement of the British Government, but, all the same, how would such people as Simon, Neville Chamberlain and the others react? Would they not begin to pour icy water on the still weak and barely rising sprigs of an Anglo-Soviet *rapprochement?* In such conditions would not the Moscow communiqué become a meaningless piece of paper?

Seeing Eden off on his departure from Moscow to Prague and Warsaw, I tried to convince myself that my doubts were groundless. But somewhere in the depths of my heart there remained a gnawing worry which gave me no rest.

These doubts proved more than justified, and subsequent events demonstrated this most clearly.

6

Churchill and Beaverbrook

However, before going on to these events, I think it essential
to deal with one substantial success which the brief thaw in Anglo-
Soviet relations brought us.

I have already said that, when he was sending me to London,
Litvinov had put before me, on the instructions of the Soviet
Government and as my most important task, the establishment
of connections and contacts with Conservative circles. I began to
act in this sense from the very first days of my work in Britain.
But up to the beginning of the thaw my efforts enjoyed a very
meagre success. I managed to 'win' Liberals, including such
important men as Lloyd George, Herbert Samuel, Archibald
Sinclair and others. The Liberals, of course, were part of the
ruling class, but in the thirties, as I have already mentioned, had
very little influence on the Government. As for Conservatives, I
had been able to establish acquaintance with some persons of the
second or third rank, but the first-class figures, as before, kept
away from the Soviet Embassy.

The only exception was the house of the Astors, but there
were special reasons for this. Lady (Nancy) Astor had in 1931
paid a visit to Moscow together with Bernard Shaw and Lord
Lothian, and had been received by the Soviet leaders, and at this
period was playing the part of a 'friend' of the U.S.S.R. Later on
I shall describe how, a few years afterwards, the same Nancy
Astor was transformed into one of the Soviet Union's worst
enemies. However, in Conservative circles Lady Astor's status
was not very high: she was considered a wealthy and unbalanced
American, capable of any extravagance, something like a political

enfant terrible. Consequently the fact that the Soviet Ambassador
kept up an acquaintance with Lady Astor was not enough to open
to him the doors of other Conservative citadels.

The coming of the thaw changed all this. Leading politicians
in the Conservative camp began to seek acquaintance with us.
Naturally I tried to utilize to the maximum the situation thus
created, and really did succeed in establishing firm contacts with a
number of the most prominent representatives of British
Conservatism—contacts so stable that they were preserved even
later, when the brief thaw in Anglo-Soviet relations gave way
first to a cooling-off and then to a real frost. The most important
and interesting of these new acquaintances were undoubtedly
Winston Churchill and Lord Beaverbrook.

At the end of July, 1934, about a month after the luncheon
with Simon which I have described, the Vansittarts invited my
wife and myself to dinner. The others present were Churchill and
his wife. The position of Churchill at this time was very peculiar.
It was already five years since he had held any Ministerial post,
and formally he remained only an ordinary M.P. The ruling
Conservative Party clearly did not wish to admit him to the
heights of authority. What was the reason?

My hypothesis amounts to the following. The ten years from
1929 to 1939 were a period of comparatively tranquil development of British political life, and the arena of public affairs was
filled by average and even petty personalities like Neville
Chamberlain, Samuel Hoare, Halifax, Simon and others. There is
no need to exaggerate Churchill's political qualities, as is often
done in western literature. Churchill not infrequently was mistaken in his assessment of people and events (I shall have to
mention this later): during the war he took a wrong line, wrong
even from the point of view of British interests in their long-term
sense: but nevertheless he was far wiser than all the personages I
have just mentioned, and in addition was distinguished by a very
strong authoritarian character. Consequently the Ministers of that
day were simply afraid of him, fearing that thanks to his qualities
and his authority in the Conservative Party and in the country he

would crush them, tie them hand and foot, transform them into his pawns. It would be better for such a grizzled political bulldog to stand aside from the road along which the chariot of power was gliding comparatively smoothly! Only the dread crisis of the second world war could bring Churchill back into the Government—to begin with as First Lord of the Admiralty, and then as Prime Minister. But here there came into play factors over which the Chamberlains and the Simons no longer had any control.

However, even without any portfolio as Minister, Churchill in those years was one of the outstanding political figures in Britain, and undoubtedly enjoyed considerable influence in wide parliamentary circles. This influence developed still further when, in the middle thirties, Churchill became leader of the internal opposition in the Conservative Party which saw the key to the safety of the British Empire in the re-creation of the Entente of the first world war.

I do not know who was responsible for the meeting between Churchill and myself, Churchill or Vansittart: but it is a fact that on that warm July evening in 1934 the six of us were seated at table talking about various current topics. When after coffee the ladies, according to British custom, withdrew to the drawing-room, and only the three men remained at table, a more serious conversation began. During this conversation Churchill frankly explained his position to me.

'The British Empire,' said Churchill, 'is my be-all and end-all. What is good for the British Empire is good for me too; what is bad for the British Empire is bad for me. . . . In 1919 I considered that the greatest danger to the British Empire was your country, and therefore I was an enemy of your country. Now I consider that the greatest danger for the British Empire is Germany, and therefore now I am an enemy of Germany. At the same time I consider that Hitler is making ready to expand not only against us but also to the east, against you. Why should we not join forces to combat our common enemy? I have been an adversary of Communism, and remain its adversary, but for the sake of the integrity of the British Empire I am ready to co-operate with the Soviets.'

I had to register that Churchill was speaking sincerely, and that the motives which he was giving for his change of direction were logical and worthy of confidence.

In the same spirit of frankness I replied to Churchill:

'Soviet people are in principle the adversaries of capitalism. But they very much want peace, and in the struggle for peace are ready to co-operate with a State founded on any system if it is genuinely striving to avert war.' And I cited a number of concrete facts and historical events to illustrate this. Churchill was quite satisfied with my words, and from that evening there began an acquaintance which was maintained until the very end of my work in Britain.

The relations between us were unusual, and even to a certain extent paradoxical. We were people of two opposite camps, and always remembered it. I also remembered that Churchill was the most important leader of intervention in 1918–20. Ideologically there lay an abyss between us. But in the sphere of foreign policy one must sometimes march together with the enemies of yesterday against the enemy of today, if interests require it. This was why in the thirties, and with full encouragement from Moscow, I maintained constant relations with Churchill in order to prepare for the joint struggle with Britain against the Hitler threat. Of course, one felt all the time that Churchill was casting about in his mind how best to use the 'Soviet factor' to preserve the world position of Great Britain. Therefore I always had to be on my guard. Nevertheless, the acquaintance with Churchill was of great value. It played its part in later events, especially in the period of the second world war.

It was somewhat otherwise that relations between myself and Lord Beaverbrook were established. In the summer of 1935, approximately a year after my first meeting with Churchill, Aneurin Bevan, the left-wing Labour Party leader, came to see me. We were well acquainted, and he came straight to the point.

'I have come to you on a delicate matter,' Bevan began. 'I have a friend, Lord Beaverbrook. You know of him, of course?'

I nodded.

'Well, Lord Beaverbrook would like to know you,' continued Bevan. 'He has already written his invitation to you to come to lunch, but asked me to find out in advance what your attitude would be. It would be unpleasant for Beaverbrook if you turned it down. . . . Besides, he really is interested to meet you on political grounds. . . . Well, what do you say?'

In recent years Beaverbrook had taken up an anti-Soviet position, and in the days of the Anglo-Soviet crisis over the Metropolitan-Vickers case had carried on a frenzied campaign against the U.S.S.R., and against me personally. . . . And now that same Beaverbrook was inviting me to lunch.

'And what are Beaverbrook's ideas and intentions now?' I asked Bevan.

'Oh, they are the very best,' said Bevan. 'Beaverbrook thinks that in the present situation Britain and Russia must go the same road.'

'Very well, then,' I replied. 'I will accept Beaverbrook's invitation. There is no point in resurrecting the past if in the present we can march together against Hitlerite Germany.'

A few days later (if my memory does not fail me it was June 4) I was sitting at table with Beaverbrook. We were alone, and I was able to study him closely. He was a short, extremely lively and restless man, with a round mobile face and acute, piercing eyes. There poured from his lips a firework torrent of wisecracks, opinions, assessments, characterizations of people and events. He did not restrain himself in his expressions. The conversation with Beaverbrook was exceptionally interesting and instructive, and I spent more than two hours with him. Several times I sought to rise and take my leave, but my host would not let me go.

In the course of the conversation Beaverbrook, like Churchill, thought it necessary to explain to me the reasons for his change of heart towards the U.S.S.R.

'Yes, yes,' he said rapidly, 'we must go together. . . . I will tell

you frankly I don't love your country very much, but I love the
British Empire. . . . For the health of the British Empire I am
ready to do anything. . . . Germany today is the main problem,
not only for Europe but for the British Empire too. So let's be
friends!'

This, too, was frank and, what was particularly important,
quite sincere. I was very pleased. I had always been revolted by
sickly sweet talk about sympathy with 'Russia and the Russian
people' with which some British politicians covered up the
emptiness of their feelings or even their anti-Soviet intrigues.
Beaverbrook's rather brutal realism was refreshing. He was
guided by the egotistical interest of his State, and was appealing
to the 'egotistical interest', as he understood it, of the Soviet
State; but on such a basis it was possible to build up a serious
policy of joint action against the common peril from the German
aggressor.

In fact, my acquaintance with Beaverbrook became much
stronger later on, and was of no little value to the Soviet Union.
In the years of the second world war Beaverbrook, as a member
of Churchill's War Cabinet, rendered no small services to our
country in matters of supply. He was also, from the very beginning of the great Patriotic War, a warm supporter of the opening
of a second front in France. It was not by chance that the Soviet
Government decorated Beaverbrook with one of our highest
Orders.

.7

It grows colder

T HE thaw in Anglo-Soviet relations did not last long—only about a year. Its highest point was Eden's visit to Moscow. Immediately afterwards there was a fall in the temperature of Anglo-Soviet relations, because the Chamberlainites were disturbed by the possibility of a stable improvement in relations between London and Moscow. They became active again, and took advantage of their political influence to begin wholesale sabotage of such a possibility.

This was the precise moment chosen by the Chamberlainites to put forward a new plan for parrying the German menace, which at that time was called the conception of 'western security'. If in 1934 the ruling circles in Britain of all trends and opinions began to be inclined to the rebirth of the Entente of the first world war, and saw in it the real guarantee for the preservation of the British Empire, now, in 1935, a division of opinion became apparent. There was a differentiation between the supporters of 'State interest' and the supporters of 'class hatred'. The first continued as before to strive for the rebirth of the Entente, and consequently for closer relations between Britain and the U.S.S.R. The others became more and more fascinated by a gamble on another horse. They argued approximately as follows: 'For the British Empire both Hitlerite Germany and Soviet Russia are dangerous. They should be incited to attack each other (all the more because the Fascists and the Communists hate each other), and we should stand aside. When Germany and the U.S.S.R. have bled each other white, and, as a result of war, have been much enfeebled, the time will come for the west to appear on the scene, and

Britain in the first place. Then the west will dictate to Germany and the U.S.S.R. the kind of peace which will ensure the security of the British Empire, and possibly its world hegemony, for a long time, if not for ever.' From this conception, naturally, there followed a struggle against *rapprochement* between London and Moscow, and also every kind of encouragement to Hitler to launch war in the east.

It was just because he took this conception into account that M. M. Litvinov, in applying the policy of the Soviet Government, put forward in the winter of 1934–5 the watchword that 'peace is indivisible', arguing that in our times any serious war in Eastern Europe must inevitably become a world war. Litvinov spoke in this sense on a number of occasions at sessions of the League of Nations and at various international conferences and meetings. He insistently argued on these lines with European statesmen and diplomats, both at official and private meetings. Sometimes he did this in minor details, too, if he thought that they could serve the interests of Soviet policy. I recall how during Eden's visit to Moscow, at the official luncheon which Maxim Maximovich organized for him, the iced pudding had inscribed on it in English: 'Peace is indivisible.' Eden did not fail to notice it.

The indivisibility of peace was also well understood by the more far-sighted among British politicians. In the spring of 1935 I was at luncheon one day with Churchill. He talked much of the Hitlerite danger, and spoke quite freely.

'What is Hitlerite Germany?' he exclaimed. 'It is a terrible and dangerous force! . . . Hitlerite Germany is a vast, scientifically organized war machine with half a dozen American gangsters at its head. You can expect anything of them. No one knows exactly what they want, and what they will be doing tomorrow. . . . Who knows what their foreign policy is? . . . I shall not be surprised at all if Hitler launches his first blow not at the U.S.S.R., because that would be fairly dangerous, but at very different countries.'

Going on then to the supporters of western security, Churchill continued:

'These people argue that just the same Germany has to fight somewhere, she must extend her dominions in some direction—so let her better carve out an empire for herself at the expense of the States in eastern and south-eastern Europe. Let her amuse herself with the Balkans or the Ukraine, but leave Britain and France alone. Such ideas are, of course, complete idiocy, but unfortunately they are still fairly popular in certain quarters of the Conservative Party. But I am firmly convinced that in the long run the victory will be not with the supporters of western security, but with those who, like Vansittart or myself, consider that peace is indivisible, and that Britain, France and the U.S.S.R. must be the backbone of the defensive alliance which will keep Germany in a wholesome state of apprehension. No concessions should be made to Hitler. Any concession on our part will be interpreted as a sign of weakness, and will only encourage Hitler to raise his demands.'

Churchill's views greatly pleased me, and I supported them in every possible way. I wanted to believe that such a man could be a good judge of the perspicacity and capacity of the British ruling class. Alas, and subsequent events showed it, Churchill displayed excessive optimism in his forecast. The Chamberlainites proved much stronger and more thick-witted than he imagined. In particular, immediately after Eden's return from Moscow they began to make vast and far from fruitless efforts to restore their influence.

The first step in this direction was the conference at Stresa in the middle of April, 1935. It was held to discuss Germany's violation of the military articles of the Versailles Treaty. Present were MacDonald and Simon from Britain, Premier Flandin and Laval (Minister of Foreign Affairs) from France, Mussolini and Suvich (Deputy Minister for Foreign Affairs) from Italy. Naturally Mussolini sabotaged any sharp action directed against Hitler, but the British and French likewise betrayed no desire to quarrel with the Nazi dictator. As a result, the Stresa conference confined itself to academic condemnation of Hitler's action, but avoided taking any effective measures against his aggressive step.

Thereby it only encouraged the Fuehrer in his further rapid progress on the same lines. More than that, the Stresa conference (particularly Simon and MacDonald) gave Mussolini to understand that Britain would not obstruct Italy in her seizure of Ethiopia, for which she was then preparing.

The next step in restoring the position of the Chamberlainites was the reconstruction of the British Government. In May, 1935, came the twenty-fifth anniversary of King George V's accession to the throne. There were many ceremonies in connection with this jubilee, and also a number of appointments. The Chamberlainites used this occasion to try to strengthen their position. The British Government preserved its previous 'National' character, but at its head there was now placed the real Prime Minister in the previous Government, the Conservative Baldwin who had previously been Deputy Premier, while the former decorative Prime Minister, MacDonald, became his deputy. Even more important were the changes which took place in the Foreign Office. By this time even in the ruling circles it had been realized that Simon's four years' management of foreign affairs had brought no benefit to the British State (no small part in this realization was played by Simon's behaviour during the Anglo-Soviet trade negotiations), and now he was shifted to the more neutral post of Home Secretary. Who would replace Simon as Foreign Secretary? A considerable struggle took place around this appointment. Vansittart very much hoped that Eden would get the post, and even worked energetically behind the scenes to this end, but the Chamberlainites strongly opposed it, and in the end were victorious.

The new Foreign Secretary was Samuel Hoare, a typical representative of the British ruling group. He had been to Oxford, at twenty-five had become Personal Private Secretary to Colonial Secretary Lyttelton, Air Minister at forty-two, Secretary for India at fifty-one and now, at fifty-five, Foreign Secretary. During the first world war Hoare was the British military agent at the Tsar's headquarters and an enthusiastic admirer of the Easter services of the Russian Orthodox Church, which he depicted very vividly in his somewhat mystical book *The Fourth Seal* (1930). There was altogether something of the mystic in Hoare's character. Thus, for example, in his drawing-room there stood a strange decorative object which had the appearance of a silvered coffin, which not infrequently aroused a slight shudder in guests who first saw it. In the middle thirties Hoare was one of the closest supporters of Chamberlain and a warm champion of western security.

However, the Chamberlainites had to reckon with the very widespread pacifist feelings in Britain at that time, which found their particularly vivid expression in the desire of the great mass of the people to ensure universal peace through the League of Nations. At the end of 1934 the British League of Nations Union, led by Lord Robert Cecil, organized a voluntary 'Peace Ballot' throughout the country, in which 11,500,000 people took part. Among them about 10,500,000 declared themselves in favour of using force against aggressors. This obliged the Chamberlainites to display a certain caution and to manœuvre. Therefore, while making Samuel Hoare Foreign Secretary, they maintained Eden as Minister without Portfolio, but with the special duty of dealing with League of Nations affairs.

The third step in the same direction was the Anglo-German Naval Agreement signed in June, 1935. The Versailles Treaty had, of course, laid down very severe restrictions on German naval armament. In February, 1935, when Hitler unilaterally swept aside all the military articles of this Treaty, he began intensive rearmament of Germany on the sea as well as on land. The conference at Stresa had condemned, albeit in a mild form, these actions of the Fuehrer. And now, only two months after Stresa, Britain officially recognized Germany's right to naval armament going far beyond the Versailles limitations! This was such a provocative act of appeasement of the aggressor that on the eve of its signature even France made a protest to Britain. However, the Baldwin Government took no account of its ally's dissatisfaction, and next day, June 18, signed the agreement. This provided that the general ratio of tonnage of the navies of the two countries should be 100 to 35, but with the right of Germany to have a submarine fleet equal to that of the entire British Empire. Semi-official commentaries left no doubt that the most important motive for concluding such an agreement was the British Government's desire to assure Germany supremacy in the Baltic against the U.S.S.R. The road for the Hitlerite armaments race was not only opened but now legally authorized.

But as in the autumn of 1935 there was to be a General Election, and the great mass of the people continued to condemn the Fascist aggressors. Samuel Hoare in September, 1935, made a sensational vote-catching speech against aggression at the League Assembly in Geneva, creating the impression that Britain was ready to apply sanctions if Italy began her war against Ethiopia. This was only a swindler's trick. For when Mussolini on October 3 did begin military operations in Africa the British ruling class did not turn a hair. And when on November 14 the election took place, and the Conservatives won a victory which was not so overwhelming as in 1931, but still ensured them a stable majority, the Chamberlainites tried to counteract Hoare's September speech. The war in Africa sharply raised the question of League of Nations sanctions against Italy. Eden displayed considerable activity in Geneva in favour of establishing sanctions, while at the same time Chamberlain in London was openly calling them 'madness'. Laval, who was now Premier in France, sabotaged the introduction of sanctions. As the U.S.S.R. was firmly defending the policy of sanctions, and as that policy was supported by a number of smaller States, Chamberlain and Laval did not succeed in completely freeing Italy from sanctions. However, they did ensure that the compromise finally adopted by the League bore a sufficiently toothless character. Sanctions, for example, were not applied to such an important strategic product as oil.

In December, 1935, the Chamberlainites took a further step forward. Samuel Hoare worked out, jointly with Laval, a plan for ending the Italo-Ethiopian war by transferring half of Ethiopia's territory to Mussolini to control. This was a frank reward to the aggressor for having committed his act of aggression, and an encouragement for other potential aggressors to follow Mussolini's example. The immediate reaction in Britain and France to the Hoare-Laval plan was such that Laval barely managed to retain his majority, while Samuel Hoare was forced to resign immediately.[1]

Only now, at last, was Eden appointed Foreign Secretary. This could be considered a success for the supporters of an Entente, but the Chamberlainites immediately surrounded the new Foreign Secretary with a number of hidden barriers which made him a prisoner of the knights of class hatred. The result could be foreseen.

When, on March 7, 1936, Hitler tore up the Locarno Treaty and reoccupied the Rhineland, and when the U.S.S.R. was proposing resolute steps against this new act of aggression the British and French Governments, supported by the United States, confined themselves to merely verbal protests, which had the same effect on Hitler as the reproaches of Krylov's cook in the fable on his cat Vaska (who 'listened, but went on eating'). Yet, as became known later, the Nazi generals who led their forces into the Rhineland had in their pockets instructions to withdraw immediately should the French offer them any resistance.

Later, when on July 18, 1936, Franco, with the active support of Hitler and Mussolini, raised a rebellion against the legitimate Government of the Spanish Republic, Britain and France—again with the support of the United States—initiated the comedy of 'non-intervention' which became in effect indirect support of Franco and his foreign protectors.[2]

---

1. However, Hoare was not long without a Ministerial post: after all, the ruling group considered him as one of themselves! He had made a slip on the question of Ethiopia, of course, but one could not long be angry with such a reliable colleague. In 1936, when public feeling had somewhat abated, Hoare was appointed First Lord of the Admiralty, and later Home Secretary.

2. I have described the details of this in my reminiscences of the Non-Intervention Committee, entitled *Spanish Notebooks*.

E

Naturally, all these activities of the British Government were in obvious contradiction to the Moscow communiqué of April 1, 1935, and in the long run bore an anti-Soviet character. Nevertheless, in the winter of 1936–7, when Baldwin was Prime Minister and Eden was Foreign Secretary, the British Government tried to maintain on the Spanish question at least the external appearance of neutrality and impartiality. I succeeded also in reducing to a minimum the hurtful consequences of our difference on Spanish affairs for Anglo-Soviet relations as a whole. I recall my conversation with Eden on this question at the very beginning of the Spanish war.

'It is clear to me,' I said, 'that the Soviet and British governments have a different approach to the Spanish events. . . . There are differences between us here which may even grow in the future: yet Spain is only one of the problems of the foreign policy of the two countries. There are many other problems, even more important, on which the U.S.S.R. and Great Britain are not in opposition. . . . Let us localize our differences on the Spanish question and do our best to prevent them injuring Anglo-Soviet relations as a whole. . . . It would be extremely undesirable for the Moscow communiqué to become a scrap of paper.'

Eden thought for a moment, and then replied:

'I quite agree with you, and will do everything possible on my part to ensure that our policy should follow the principles set forth in the Moscow communiqué. . . . It is very important not only for Britain and the U.S.S.R., it is also important in the interests of general peace.' He was silent again for a moment, and then added, somewhat more quietly: 'But you understand that this does not depend upon me alone.'

I understood this very well: but nevertheless I must put on record that up to the middle of 1937 the temperature of Anglo-Soviet relations was considerably above zero.

8

Below freezing point

ON MAY 28, 1937, Premier Baldwin retired, and Neville Chamberlain became head of the Government in his place. Learning this news, I could not help but think: 'Churchill was mistaken in his forecast. Not he but Chamberlain has taken the helm. Now there is the prospect of an agreement between Chamberlain and Hitler—and what next?'

Neville Chamberlain was undoubtedly the most sinister figure on the political horizon of Britain at that time. Sinister for the profound and innate reactionary character of his views, sinister for the influence which he enjoyed in the Conservative Party. The fact that Neville Chamberlain was a man of narrow views and small capabilities, that his political horizon, to use Lloyd George's expression, did not rise above that of 'a provincial manufacturer of iron bedsteads', only increased the danger of his remaining in power. Neville's father, the famous Joseph Chamberlain, considered this son, unlike his other son Austen, unsuited to politics, and from his youth trained him for commerce. However, on the commercial field likewise, Neville won no particular laurels. Then he was launched on a 'municipal career'. Here, after a series of intermediate stages, he ultimately became Lord Mayor of Birmingham. In 1917, as a Conservative of distinguished origin, Neville Chamberlain was given the post of Director of National Service in Lloyd George's Coalition Cabinet, but was an utter failure and was expelled from the Government. And now this same Neville Chamberlain had become head of the British Cabinet, in the midst, moreover, of a complicated and difficult

67

world situation. Involuntarily the thought came to mind: 'What a profound demoralization of the British ruling class!'

For me, as Ambassador of the Soviet Union, Neville Chamberlain's appointment was of quite particular significance. I had not forgotten my conversation with him in November, 1932, which I have mentioned earlier. The next five years had completely confirmed, by many facts and examples, that Neville Chamberlain was a consistent enemy of our country. Such a Prime Minister could make Anglo-Soviet relations only more tense and just because of his hostility to the Soviet State could only reinforce the policy of appeasing the aggressors. We could expect nothing good of him.

However gloomy my feelings, I decided all the same to visit the new Premier and probe his state of mind. He received me in his room in the House of Commons on July 29. This time Chamberlain was more calm and restrained than during our first encounter five years before. I asked him about the general outlines of policy which the British Government intended to follow in the sphere of international relations. Chamberlain explained to me long and patiently that the main problem at the moment, in his opinion, was Germany. If this question were settled first all other questions would present no particular difficulty. But how was the German problem to be settled? This seemed quite possible to the Prime Minister if the proper method of settlement were applied.

'If we could sit down with the Germans at a table,' he said, 'and pencil in hand go through all their complaints and their claims, this would greatly clear up relations.'

So the whole problem was one of sitting down at a table pencil in hand! How simple! I could not help recalling Lloyd George's words about 'a provincial manufacturer of iron bedsteads'. He did evidently really see Hitler and himself as two merchants who would, in the event of a dispute, argue, chaff and then in the end strike a bargain. So primitive were the Prime Minister's political conceptions.

From all that Chamberlain said to me on July 29 it followed

beyond doubt that his aspirations were centred on a Four-Power (Western) Pact, and that the road to it would be the appeasement of Hitler and Mussolini in every possible way.

This pessimistic forecast became even more probable thanks to the fact that it was just at this time there was finally formed in London the so-called Cliveden set, which played such a sinister role in the years before the second world war. Lady (Nancy) Astor, the same Lady Astor who in 1932–3 had coquetted with 'friendship' towards the Soviet Union, during the subsequent years revealed her real face, and became in the end the 'hostess' of a political salon in which the most reactionary representatives of the Conservative Party regularly gathered. Usually at week-ends in her luxurious mansion at Cliveden, near London, which she tried to make into an imitation of Versailles, such people as Neville Chamberlain, Lord Halifax, Samuel Hoare, Kingsley Wood and others met together. Here they ate and drank, amused themselves, exchanged opinions and projected their plans for immediate action. Not infrequently most important affairs of State were decided between two rounds of golf. The closer war came, the more active did Cliveden become. Lady Astor's salon became the main citadel of the enemies of the Soviet Union and the friends of an Anglo-German *rapprochement*. From here came the most energetic propaganda for the conception of western security; here they pictured to themselves with particular delight the prospect of mutual destruction by the Soviet Union and Germany, on the fulfilment of which the frequenters of Cliveden had put their money. Lady Astor's salon had very great influence on the appointment of Ministers, the formation of governments and the determination of the policy of those governments. The coming to power of Neville Chamberlain heralded such power for the Cliveden set as might give rise to the most anxious apprehension among the leaders of the Soviet Union. In any case there was not long to wait.

Chamberlain's main aim was the appeasement of the Fascist dictators with a view to establishing western security. This, of course, was idiocy, as Churchill had put it: but in Chamberlain (and not only in Chamberlain) class hatred towards the country of Socialism was so great that it completely clouded the normal process of reason. Churchill in his war memoirs, when speaking of Chamberlain and his attitude to Hitler, ironically remarks: 'Chamberlain had cherished the hope of appeasing and reforming him and leading him to grace.'[1] In this passage Churchill observes the literary decencies. In private conversations he expressed himself much more strongly. I remember how once he said to me: 'Neville is a fool. . . . He thinks he can ride the tiger.'

Unfortunately, that was precisely what Chamberlain thought, and that is why he became the consistent apostle of the policy of appeasing the aggressors. In order to carry through such a policy in practice he needed a government constituted in harmony with this idea—and above all a 'suitable' Foreign Secretary. Eden was not suitable for this purpose, all the more so because he was extremely unpopular in Rome and in Berlin. Chamberlain's selection for this key post was Lord Halifax; but taking into account public opinion then prevailing, the Premier did not venture to get rid of Eden immediately. The ground had to be prepared beforehand, and it would be best of all if Eden could be compelled to resign. Therefore Chamberlain, for the time being, appointed Lord Halifax to the honourable but purely decorative post of Lord Privy Seal—once again a Minister without Portfolio who would be given particular work to do. And, as we shall see later, the most important special work which Halifax received was of an external political character.

Chamberlain's first striking action in the sphere of appeasement of the dictators was the dispatch of a friendly letter to Mussolini, to which Mussolini, of course, replied without delay with just as friendly a letter. Then Chamberlain began energetic negotiations with him aiming at the conclusion of a far-reaching treaty of friendship and co-operation between Britain and Italy. Eden and some other prominent politicians opposed these negotiations— not because they sympathized with the Spanish Republic. Not at all! Neither Eden nor most of his sympathizers cherished any

1. *The Second World War*, Vol. 1, page 281 (1948).

friendly feelings for the Spanish Republic. But they realized the perfidy of the Fascist dictators, had little belief in their promises and therefore demanded that, in order to prove that his intentions were serious, Mussolini should first withdraw from Spain his troops fighting on Franco's side. But Chamberlain would listen to nothing, and stubbornly pursued his policy of signing an Anglo-Italian agreement as rapidly as possible. This was the basis for the clash between Chamberlain and Eden (possibly artificially blown up by the Prime Minister) as a result of which, on February 20, 1938, Eden resigned. With him resigned his Parliamentary Under-Secretary, Lord Cranborne, who in those years was also a supporter of *rapprochement* with the U.S.S.R. Shortly before this, on January 1, 1938, Vansittart had been removed from active participation in the Foreign Office and appointed to the honourable but not very operational post of Chief Diplomatic Adviser to the Government. Telling me of his new title, Vansittart remarked with a wry smile: 'Chief Diplomatic Adviser. . . . But you are not obliged to take his advice. . . . Everything depends on what the Prime Minister wants.'

Vansittart anticipated his future very well. Chamberlain really did not turn to him for advice.

Now the genuine and ever more powerful adviser of the Prime Minister on foreign affairs began rapidly to come into prominence: Sir Horace Wilson. I knew him well, from the days of the trade negotiations with Great Britain. At that time Horace Wilson, bearing the title of Chief Industrial Adviser of the Government, was the main figure on the British side in working out the Temporary Trade Agreement of 1934. Wilson was well acquainted with everything pertaining to trade and industry, but his horizon in foreign affairs did not extend beyond that of the man in the street. And Chamberlain was making such a man his most trusted expert in settling the most important international problems. It seemed like madness. . . . But was not all Chamberlain's foreign policy one unbroken madness, fermented in the yeast of class hatred, stupidity and illiteracy?

Having cleansed the Foreign Office of people whom he found

embarrassing, Chamberlain now appointed Lord Halifax as Foreign Secretary. He was a British aristocrat of ancient lineage who had gone through a long political and administrative career, culminating in the post of Viceroy of India. Tall, gaunt, slow-moving, a black glove on his injured left hand, he spoke in a calm, low voice, always preserving a pleasant smile. Externally he attracted one's sympathy, and gave the impression of a profound thinker, or at any rate of a man interested in great problems. His turn of mind was philosophical: but the philosophy close to his heart was a mystical religious one. He belonged to the 'High Church' current in Anglican thought, and liked talking on moral and religious themes. It was said that when Halifax was Viceroy of India there was a small chapel behind his study. Before any serious meetings or discussions he would withdraw for a few minutes to ask God to enlighten his reason. Halifax undoubtedly was a widely cultivated man—but this did not prevent him (we shall see examples later) from displaying a complete misunderstanding of the present day and the motive forces of our epoch. But this was a clear sign of the limitations of his class outlook.

As a member of Chamberlain's Government, Halifax supported in every way the policy of appeasement and was one of the pillars of the Cliveden set. Temperamentally Halifax was easy to get on with, and he put up without difficulty with the fact that the Prime Minister, together with Horace Wilson, usurped control of British foreign policy, and reduced the Foreign Office to the condition of a mere diplomatic chancery attached to his own person. To avoid any complications, the important post of Permanent Under-Secretary for Foreign Affairs, taken from Vansittart, was given to Alexander Cadogan, who could be relied upon not to provide any unexpected surprises.

Having in this way assured himself of a retiring and submissive machinery, Chamberlain now set about the systematic realization of his own foreign policy.

It began with Germany. At the end of November, 1937, Halifax had already received from Chamberlain instructions to make a pilgrimage to Berlin and to enter upon negotiations with

Hitler for a general regulation of Anglo-German relations. At that time we did not yet know all the details of these negotiations, but their general sense was clear to us; and, moreover, a little of what had taken place in Berlin leaked out into British political circles and became known to us. As a result, distrust on the Soviet side to Chamberlain's Government very much increased. Today the materials of the German Ministry for Foreign Affairs captured by the Soviet Army in Berlin show that there were more than sufficient grounds for our distrust.

In fact, the record of the conversation between Hitler and Halifax on November 17, 1937, published by the U.S.S.R. Foreign Ministry in 1948, makes it quite clear that Halifax, on behalf of the British Government, offered Hitler a kind of alliance on the basis of the 'Pact of Four' and a free hand in Central and Eastern Europe. In particular, Halifax stated that 'no possibility of changing the existing situation must be precluded', and later on made this more precise by saying that 'to these questions belong Danzig, Austria and Czechoslovakia'. Of course, in pointing out to Hitler a direction in which his aggressions would meet least resistance from the Chamberlain Government, Halifax thought it essential to make the pious reservation:

'England was only interested that any alterations should be effected by peaceful evolution, so as to avoid methods which might cause far-reaching disturbances which were not desired either by the Fuehrer or by other countries.'[1]

However, Hitler understood the value of this reservation very well, and therefore could consider his conversation with Halifax as London's blessing for the violent seizure of 'living space' in the regions indicated. And when Eden resigned, and Halifax became Foreign Secretary, Hitler had good grounds for deciding that the time had come to put into effect the programme of aggression which had been sketched out in the conversation between them in November, 1937. He lost no time. On March 12, 1938, twelve days after the appointment of Halifax as Foreign

1. *Documents and Materials Relating to the Eve of the Second World War*, Vol. I (Moscow, 1948), pp. 20, 25, 34 (English edition).

Secretary, he made his first big leap, occupying Austria with a lightning blow. As though jeering at the London appeasers, the Fuehrer timed his aggression for the very day when Chamberlain was ceremoniously receiving Ribbentrop, the German Minister for Foreign Affairs, who had come to Britain. And what happened? Britain and France reacted to this outrageous act of aggression by purely verbal protests which neither they themselves, and still less Hitler, took seriously.

However great and legitimate, after all that had happened, was the Soviet Government's mistrust of the Chamberlain Government, nevertheless at this critical moment the leaders of the U.S.S.R. made an attempt to appeal to the common sense of the leaders of Great Britain. On March 17, 1938, five days after the seizure of Austria, M. M. Litvinov, on behalf of the Soviet Government, gave an interview in Moscow to representatives of the press in the course of which he said:

'While previous cases of aggression took place in continents more or less remote from Europe or on the outskirts of Europe ... the outrage on this occasion has been committed in the centre of Europe and has created an undoubted danger, not only to the eleven countries now bordering the aggressor but for all European States, and not only European. . . .

'First and foremost arises the threat to Czechoslovakia. . . .

'The present international situation puts before all peaceable States, and big States in particular, the question of their responsibility for the subsequent destinies of the peoples of Europe, and not only of Europe. The Soviet Government is aware of its share in this responsibility; it is aware of the obligations incumbent upon it under the League Covenant, the Briand-Kellogg Pact and the treaties of mutual assistance it has concluded with France and Czechoslovakia; and I can say on behalf of the Government that, for its part, it is ready as before to join in collective action which, decided jointly, would have the purpose of arresting the further development of aggression and removing the accentuated danger of a new world shambles. It agrees to proceed immediately to discuss practical measures dictated by the circumstances with other Powers in the League of Nations or outside it.'

At the same time I received from Moscow the instruction to transmit the text of the interview to the British Government, with an accompanying Note to the effect that this interview was the official expression of the point of view of the Soviet Government. I did this. The same was done, also by instructions from Moscow, by the Soviet Ambassadors in Paris and Washington. In this way the U.S.S.R. publicly proclaimed its readiness to take energetic measures against aggression, and called upon Britain, France and the U.S.A. to do the same. The Soviet Union did its duty. But what about its partners?

On March 24 the British Foreign Office sent the Soviet Embassy a long Note signed by Halifax. It stated that the British Government would warmly welcome the assembly of an international conference, at which it might be expected that all European States would consent to be represented' (i.e. both aggressors and non-aggressors—I.M.), but that it objected to the calling of 'a conference only attended by some of the European Powers, and designed . . . to organize concerted action against aggression'. For, in the opinion of the British Government, such a conference would not have a favourable effect upon the prospects of European peace.[1]

And so, instead of a struggle against the aggressors, there were to be aimless conversations with the aggressors. One more Non-Intervention Committee, but this time on European affairs, not merely Spain! In other words, tranquillizing pills for the mass of the people in order to give the aggressors time to prepare for new 'leaps'. This is what the British Government wanted. This is how in practice it deciphered Halifax's words about the desirability of changes in the European situation by 'peaceful evolution'.

The response to the Soviet approach in Paris and Washington was no better than it had been in London.

It might have seemed that the seizure of Austria should have

1. *Documents on British Foreign Policy, 1919–1939*, Third Series, Vol. 1, p. 101.

at least to some extent brought Chamberlain to his senses, and
made him more careful in his relations with the Fascist dictators.
Far from it. Blinded with hatred of the Soviet Union, Chamberlain would see nothing else. He stubbornly continued his fatal
policy (fatal for Britain herself), and on April 16 signed the
agreement for friendship and collaboration with Italy which he
had so passionately sought. This agreement included recognition
by the British Government of Italy's annexation of Ethiopia.
Wishing, however, to calm somewhat the democratic elements in
Britain, who considered the conclusion of an Anglo-Italian
agreement at such a time to be betrayal of the Spanish Republic,
Chamberlain made one important reservation. He undertook to
ratify the treaty only after Italy had evacuated her troops from
Spain, in keeping with the plan which was then being worked out
by the Non-Intervention Committee. Later I shall describe how
Chamberlain fulfilled this obligation.

In the spring of 1938 I met Lady Vansittart at a diplomatic
reception. She was very depressed. Her husband's elimination
from any active part in British foreign policy, the appointment
of Halifax as Foreign Secretary, the domination of Clivedenites
in the Government and much else made her very pessimistic.

'Van is convinced,' she said, 'that war is very close, just round
the corner. . . . What a misfortune that we have such a bad Prime
Minister at such a difficult time!'

Then she began to ask me about the state of Anglo-Soviet
relations. I quite frankly told her how matters stood. She wrung
her hands and said:

'And don't you remember how four years ago Van succeeded
in improving relations between our two countries? . . . But all
that's been spoiled now.'

I replied: 'Yes, in 1934–5, with the help of your husband, there
was a thaw in Anglo-Soviet relations—but now their temperature
is below zero.'

Lady Vansittart again wrung her hands, and said with deep feeling:
'At all events, Van has done all he could.'

9

Munich

But if Chamberlain was not able to draw any lesson from the overthrow of Austria, Hitler proved a much more capable pupil. The 'leap' at Vienna was an important probe for him. The Nazi dictator wanted to test how the democratic Powers would react to his aggression. The test demonstrated that Britain and France did not move. It was not surprising that Hitler interpreted this as meaning that the way was open. Accordingly, two months after the annexation of Austria, he began a new and still more serious operation.

What Litvinov had foretold in his interview of March 17 came to pass: the storm-cloud appeared over Czechoslovakia. In May, 1938, Hitler launched a furious campaign against that country, and not only in the press and on the radio: German troops began to mass on its borders, and the Sudeten Nazis within, on orders from Berlin, began the most impudent provocations against the Czechoslovak Government. The political atmosphere in Czechoslovakia, Central Europe, Britain and France became more and more tense. There was a smell of gunpowder. After all, France had a pact of mutual assistance with Czechoslovakia, and if the latter were attacked by Germany, France would be bound to come to her aid. Britain had no such formal pact with Czechoslovakia, but as the close ally of France, she too could not have stood aside. By August the situation had become so menacing, and the alarm and anxiety of the masses in France and Britain so great, that the British Government was obliged to do something to relieve the tension created. What did it do? Something entirely in Chamberlain's style.

Instead of firmly stating that Britain and France would not allow Hitler to swallow Czechoslovakia—a step which still had some chance of arresting the hand of the aggressor—the Chamberlain Government decided to send to Czechoslovakia a mission headed by Lord Runciman. Lord Runciman was an elderly magnate who had never taken part in international affairs—deaf, ponderous and even somewhat ignorant of where Czechoslovakia was (I discovered this in a conversation with him in the summer of 1938). Officially the Runciman mission was to 'investigate' the situation on the spot and make proposals for mediation with the purpose of settling the German-Czechoslovak conflict. In reality, however, as events proved, the mission's work reduced itself to opening the way for the dismemberment of Czechoslovakia.

Although the reception given in London and Paris to the Soviet *démarche* of March 17, 1938, after the occupation of Austria, was far from encouraging further attempts of the same nature, the Soviet Government, in view of the terrible peril to Czechoslovakia, decided once again to appeal to the common sense of the French and British leaders. We thought: 'Perhaps the bitter experience of the months since then has taught them something. . . . Perhaps even now they may be ready for more energetic action against the aggressors. . . . Not a single possibility, even the smallest, must be allowed to go by for averting disaster.'

Out of such considerations, Litvinov on September 2, 1938, informed Payart, the French *chargé d'affaires* in Moscow (Ambassador Naggiar was away), and asked him urgently to transmit to the French Government that the Government of the U.S.S.R. in the event of a German attack on Czechoslovakia would fulfil its obligations under the Soviet-Czechoslovak Pact of Mutual Assistance of 1935, and would give armed assistance to Czechoslovakia. But as, under this Pact, the obligation to give aid entered into force only if at the same time France, bound to Czechoslovakia by a similar Pact, took up arms against Germany, the Government of the U.S.S.R. would like to know the intentions of the French Government in the situation thus created. For its part, the Government of the U.S.S.R. was inviting the French Government immediately to arrange a consultation between representatives of the Soviet, French and Czechoslovak General Staffs to work out the necessary measures. Litvinov thought Rumania would allow Soviet troops and aircraft transit through its territory, but considered it very desirable, in order to influence Rumania in this sense, to put the question of eventual aid to Czechoslovakia before the League of Nations as soon as possible. If there were even a majority in the League Council in favour of such aid (strictly according to the Covenant, unanimity was required) Rumania would undoubtedly support it, and would not object to Soviet forces passing through its territory.

It was approximately at the same time, as Gottwald (who became President of Czechoslovakia after the war) subsequently revealed, that J. V. Stalin through him informed the then President Benes that the Soviet Union was ready to afford armed assistance to Czechoslovakia even if France did not do so.

On the morning of September 3 I received from Moscow a telegram containing the statement made by Litvinov to Payart. In the circumstances of that day it was a document of the greatest political significance. The important thing was that it should become as widely known as possible, because the Cliveden set had all through August carried on a whispering campaign in political circles to the following effect: 'We should be glad to save Czechoslovakia, but it is hard to do this without Russia, and Russia is keeping quiet and obviously evading the fulfilment of its obligations under the Soviet-Czechoslovak Pact of Mutual Assistance.'

The same day, September 3, I visited Churchill at his country house, Chartwell, and told him in detail of Litvinov's statement to Payart. Churchill at once realized its importance and said that he would immediately inform Halifax of my communication. He fulfilled his promise; that same day, September 3, he sent Halifax a letter conveying in detail Litvinov's *démarche*. He confirms this in his own war memoirs.[1] Not confining myself to the conversation with Churchill, I also met Lloyd George and Arthur Greenwood, Deputy Leader of the Labour Party, and repeated to them what I had told Churchill.

My calculation in doing so was that the three Opposition leaders would undoubtedly tell their party colleagues of Litvinov's *démarche* (all the more so because when informing them of it I did not ask them to keep it a secret) and consequently political circles in London would know the real attitude of the U.S.S.R. in such a burning issue. If any member of the Government were to begin slanderous talk in Parliament about the 'passivity' of the U.S.S.R. on the Czechoslovak question there could be a reply from the Opposition restoring the true facts. Subsequently my calculation was justified completely.

I did not doubt then, and do not doubt today, that if the French Government had grasped the Soviet hand stretched out to it on September 2, if Britain and France even at that late hour had sincerely accepted joint action with the U.S.S.R., Czecho-

1. Churchill writes: 'In the afternoon of September 2 I received a message from the Soviet Ambassador that he would like to come down to Chartwell and see me at once upon a matter of urgency. . . . I thereupon received the Ambassador, and after a few preliminaries he told me in precise and formal detail the story set out below. Before he had got very far I realized that he was making a declaration to me, a private person, because the Soviet Government preferred this channel to a direct offer to the Foreign Office, which might have encountered a rebuff. It was clearly intended that I should report what I was told to His Majesty's Government. This was not actually stated by the Ambassador, but it was implied by the fact that no request for secrecy was made. As the matter struck me at once as being of the first importance, I was careful not to prejudice its consideration by Halifax and Chamberlain by proceeding to commit myself in any way, or use language which would excite controversy between us.' Churchill then goes on to give the text of his letter to Halifax in which he sets out very precisely what I told him then of Litvinov's talk with Payart (*The Second World War*, Vol. 1, pp. 229–30).

As can be seen from the text, the circumstances and motives which impelled me to approach Churchill in this case were somewhat different from those by which he explains my action, but the fact of my communication itself is set forth correctly.

slovakia would have been saved, and the whole later course of European and world events would have taken a different direction. But to act in this way would have meant a quarrel with Hitler, burying the plans for western security, renouncing the hope of a clash between Germany and the U.S.S.R. . . . Neither Chamberlain nor Daladier would accept this. They preferred to cherish their stupid and fantastic chimeras, dictated by class hatred of the country of Socialism. They were ready thereby to sacrifice Czechoslovakia, and not only Czechoslovakia. . . .

Churchill in his memoirs tells how he received a reply on September 5, in which the Foreign Secretary stated that putting the question of Czechoslovakia before the League of Nations at present would not be 'helpful, but that he would keep it in his mind'.

Two days after Halifax's reply to Churchill there appeared a sinister leading article in *The Times* (September 7) which patently indicated that the best way out of the situation would be the transfer of the Sudeten districts by Czechoslovakia to Germany. The British Foreign Office hastened to state that it had nothing to do with this leading article—but nobody believed this.

I remember how the following day, September 8, Halifax invited me to see him, and in the course of conversation on various subjects stated that the British Government had no connection with the newspaper's statement—but I did not believe him either. Of course, I allowed for the possibility that neither the Foreign Office nor the Government as a whole had given *The Times* any direct and formal instructions to print this unfortunate leading article. But had the highest authorities any lack of indirect and unofficial ways of ensuring an expression of the opinions and views they desired in the press? And that is how matters stood in this particular case, since the whole content and tone of *The Times* leading article perfectly reflected in spirit the ideas and actions of the Cliveden set. What justification, then, would I have had for believing Halifax's denial?

Then followed the shameful days of Munich. The head of the British Government, the 'man with the umbrella', as the

F

newspaper wits christened him in those days, with the energetic support of Daladier sank to the role of a kind of second-rate political commercial traveller, convulsively flitting between Hitler and the Czechoslovak Government. More than this: Chamberlain humiliated himself to the point of becoming the 'big stick' of the Nazi leader, demanding that Czechoslovakia should capitulate to the German aggressor.

However, before these efforts were crowned finally with success, the U.S.S.R. made one more attempt to save the situation. In September, 1938, the League of Nations Assembly was held as usual. Litvinov came to Geneva. He called me over from London to take part in the work of the Soviet delegation. The atmosphere in Geneva was extremely tense. There were the most alarming rumours and reports in the League corridors. An attack by Germany on Czechoslovakia was expected any day. Even the peaceful Swiss were carrying out anti-aircraft exercises and arranging trial black-outs.

In Geneva we learned that the French Foreign Minister, Bonnet, one of the most malignant enemies of the U.S.S.R., had concealed Litvinov's statement to Payart from the majority of the members of the French Government. Bonnet was constantly explaining the treacherous policy of the French Government in relation to Czechoslovakia by 'the passivity of Russia' on this subject, and the statement of the Soviet People's Commissar of September 2 did not suit him at all. Now it turned out that no one in France knew of the Soviet Government's readiness to come to the aid of Czechoslovakia—and that included the members of her Government. It was essential to show France and the whole world what the true attitude of the U.S.S.R. was. It was just for this reason that Litvinov, in his speech of September 21, 1938, from the rostrum of the League of Nations, openly repeated what he had communicated to the French Government nineteen days before by diplomatic channels through Payart. Bonnet's intrigue had failed, and its exposure to the whole world helped to strengthen the international authority of the U.S.S.R.

Two days later, on September 23, the British representatives in Geneva, Mr. R. A. Butler and Lord de la Warr, asked Litvinov and myself to have a talk on the situation. The British wanted to know how the Soviet side conceived of the practical steps needed to follow up Litvinov's statement of two days before at the League. In reply Litvinov suggested that a conference should be called immediately of representatives of Britain, France and the U.S.S.R. in Paris or in some other suitable place (not Geneva) to work out measures for defending Czechoslovakia. He added that the Soviet-Czechoslovak Pact of Mutual Assistance would be put into effect irrespective of what attitude the League of Nations took up (such a statement had been made to the Czechoslovak Government three days before, in reply to an enquiry by the latter as to the attitude of the Soviet Government). Furthermore Litvinov informed them that the Soviet Government had given a serious warning to the Government of Poland: if Warsaw were to attack Czechoslovakia in order to seize the Tešin region (about which there was a lot of talk at the time) the U.S.S.R. would consider the Soviet-Polish Pact of Non-Aggression automatically annulled.

Butler and de la Warr seemed very interested in Litvinov's statements, and even displayed something like semi-sympathy with the actions of the U.S.S.R. They promised that they would immediately report our conversation to London, and on receipt of instructions would meet us again. . . . Alas, this further meeting never took place (naturally, through no fault of ours). And how could it be otherwise? It was just in these last days of September, 1938, that Chamberlain and Daladier were rounding off their 'Operation Treachery' against Czechoslovakia.

On September 27 Litvinov asked me to go back to London immediately. 'Your presence there just now is much more important than in Switzerland,' he said.

The same day I left Geneva. It was pitch-dark at the station, because the local authorities that evening had arranged a trial blackout. Early in the morning of the 28th I was in Paris. It was raining, and the familiar streets of the French capital were deserted and melancholy. I arrived the same day in London at about 4 p.m., and went straight from the station to Parliament. I had arrived at the most dramatic moment.

It will be known that Chamberlain's first pilgrimage to Hitler was on September 15. Hitler received the British Prime Minister at Berchtesgaden, and set out his demands on Czechoslovakia, threatening to use force if the latter refused. Chamberlain returned to London. There was a special conference of the British and French Ministers, which accepted Hitler's demands. On September 19, under pressure from London and Paris, the Czechoslovak Government also accepted these demands.[1] Thereupon Chamberlain flew for a second time to see Hitler.

The meeting took place at Godesberg on September 22 and 23. Chamberlain had reckoned that when he laid Czechoslovakia's agreement on the table he would earn the approval of the Fuehrer —but he was cruelly undeceived. Realizing at Berchtesgaden that he was faced not with a steel-clad knight but with a rag-stuffed 'man with an umbrella', Hitler decided that there was no call for restraint. At the second meeting with Chamberlain in Godesberg he put forward new demands, much more harsh than at Berchtesgaden. The British Prime Minister was very much discouraged, but nevertheless undertook to 'persuade' Czechoslovakia to yield once again. He returned to London, and together with Daladier attempted for the second time to exercise pressure on Prague. But here his attempt misfired: the Czechoslovak Government rejected Hitler's Godesberg programme. In making up their minds the Czechoslovaks were influenced a good deal by the assurance received from the Soviet Union a few days before that it was ready to afford Czechoslovakia assistance in any conditions, even should France betray her.

Hitler was infuriated, and declared on September 26 that if Czechoslovakia had not capitulated by 2 p.m. on the 28th he would open hostilities. Chamberlain and Daladier were panic-stricken, and the British Prime Minister made a most obsequious

1. The top group of the Czechoslovak bourgeoisie, including Benes and a number of members of the Government, were inclined to capitulation, which considerably assisted Chamberlain and Daladier in their task.

appeal to Hitler and Mussolini to arrange a Four-Power meeting in order finally to settle the Czechoslovak question. At the same time, in order to arouse suitable feelings among the mass of the population, the French Government issued orders calling up several contingents of reservists, while the British Government mobilized the Fleet and adopted some measures of anti-aircraft defence. All were waiting in a terrible state of tension: would Hitler agree or not agree to a new meeting?

When on September 28 I sat down in my place in the Diplomatic Gallery of the House of Commons, Chamberlain, visibly excited, was standing before the Government bench and nervously waving his right hand, showing everyone a sheet of white paper he was holding. It was a letter from Hitler, just received during the meeting, in reply to Chamberlain's tearful petition for a meeting of the Four. Hitler had agreed. Chamberlain did not conceal his delight. The vast majority of the Conservatives gave him a real ovation. The Labour and Liberal M.P.s were more restrained, but also did not conceal their joy. It was amid these scenes that Chamberlain left the Chamber in order at once to begin his journey to Munich

The whole scene produced the most painful impression on me. It was as though you could see a heavy coach, packed with people, rolling down an inclined plane into an abyss, and could do nothing to stop it. When I came down from the Gallery into the Lobby I met one of my Labour acquaintances whom I had seen applauding Chamberlain.

'Why were you applauding?' I asked him.

'Well, why ever not?' he replied. 'After all, Czechoslovakia has been saved, and there won't be any war.'

I replied: 'I don't want to be a Cassandra, but remember my words: Czechoslovakia is lost, and war has become inevitable.'

The M.P. looked at me with amazement. 'Do you mean that seriously?' he asked in surprise.

'Quite seriously. . . . You will see.'

What happened after that is well known. On September 29 and 30 the Munich conference was held. Hitler behaved with extreme

insolence, and Mussolini supported him. Chamberlain and
Daladier wriggled like eels. In the end, behind the back of
Czechoslovakia, the Munich Agreement was signed.

The essence of this was that the Sudeten districts were transferred to Germany with all the property they contained, and in
addition Czechoslovakia had to satisfy the territorial demands
made on her by Poland and Hungary. The rest of Czechoslovakia,
defenceless and humiliated, was to receive a guarantee from the
Big Four—a guarantee the value of which, after all that had
happened, was little more than zero.

In order to some extent to weaken the painful impression
which the Munich betrayal was bound to make on British public
opinion, Chamberlain persuaded Hitler to sign with him a paper
to the effect that henceforth there should be no wars between
Britain and Germany. It was a valueless promise destined, as the
future proved, only for the wastepaper basket. It was this scrap
of paper which Chamberlain demonstratively waved at London
Airport on his return from Munich, proclaiming loudly that now
'peace in our time' was assured.

Lord Halifax kept abreast of his Prime Minister. The German
Ambassador in Britain, von Dirksen, recording his conversation
with the Foreign Secretary on August 9, 1939, states among other
things:

'In the further course of the conversation Lord Halifax said
that he would now like to give me an exact picture of his ideas and
views as they had stood after Munich. . . . After Munich he had
been persuaded that fifty years of world peace were now assured,
roughly on the following basis: Germany the dominating power
on the Continent, with predominant rights in South-Eastern
Europe, particularly in the field of commercial policy; Britain
would engage only in moderate trade in that area; in Western
Europe, Britain and France protected from conflicts with
Germany by the lines of fortification on both sides and endeav-
ouring to retain and develop their possessions by defensive means;
friendship with America; friendship with Portugal; Spain for the
time being an indefinite factor which for the next few years at

least would necessarily have to hold aloof from all combinations
of Powers;[1] Russia an out-of-the-way, vast and scarcely survey-
able territory; Britain bent on safeguarding her Mediterranean
communications with the Dominions and the Far East, via Aden,
Colombo and Singapore.'[2]

When one reads these lines it is difficult to say whether they
spoke more of imperialist malice or phenomenal historical blindness. One thing is clear: Halifax did not in the least understand
what was going on in the world. How characteristic, in particular,
his remark about Russia! He could find nothing more intelligent
to say about a people inhabiting one-sixth of the world, and
which had become the herald of the future of mankind.

The reaction to the Munich Agreement in Britain was a very
stormy one. Wide masses of the people, who better understood
what was what than Halifax did, were indignant at the betrayal
of Czechoslovakia and alarmed at the ever-nearing and growing
peril of war. More far-sighted circles in the ruling class understood
the abyss into which the country was being dragged by its Prime
Minister, and experienced a feeling of profound humiliation at the
pitiful role he had played in all this tragic affair. One member of
the Government itself was found—First Lord of the Admiralty
Duff Cooper—who could not swallow what had happened, and
on October 1, 1938, demonstratively resigned. However, the
Cliveden set only closed its ranks more firmly, and made an
attempt to shift responsibility for its historic crime on to the
shoulders of the . . . Soviet Union! In the light of all narrated
earlier this may seem fantastic imbecility, yet nevertheless it
was so.

On October 11, 1938, ten days after the Munich betrayal, Lord
Winterton, a member of the Government, made a public speech
in which he explained that concessions by the British and French
to Hitler were inevitable. Why? Because of the military weakness
of the Soviet Union and its inability and therefore unwillingness

1. At the time of Munich the war was still going on in Spain.
2. *Documents and Materials Relating to the Eve of the Second World War*
(English edition, Moscow, 1948), Vol. II, pp. 128–9.

to fulfil its obligations under the Pact of Mutual Assistance with Czechoslovakia.

When I read Winterton's speech in the newspapers I was very indignant and asked at once to be received by Halifax, to whom I made a protest against Winterton's slanderous invention. At the same time I made a statement to the press on behalf of the Soviet Embassy, in which I said:

'This statement of Lord Winterton's is a complete perversion of the actual position of the U.S.S.R., which was explicitly, and without leaving any room for misunderstanding, stated by the People's Commissar for Foreign Affairs, M. Litvinov, in his speech at Geneva on September 21. In this speech M. Litvinov recapitulated his conversation with the French *chargé d'affaires* in Moscow on September 2, in which, on behalf of the Soviet Government, he declared that the U.S.S.R. intended to fulfil all its obligations under the Soviet-Czechoslovak Pact and, together with France, would afford assistance to Czechoslovakia by the ways open to the U.S.S.R. He added that the Soviet War Department was ready to start immediate staff talks with the representatives of the French and Czechoslovak War Departments in order to discuss measures appropriate to the moment.'

I thought that matters would end there. But no, the following morning, October 12, I read in the newspapers the report of a new public speech by Winterton, in which he repeated his lying assertion. This finally enraged me, and I gave the press a second and sharper statement by the Embassy, in which I said that it was useless to argue with a man who deliberately shut his eyes to the real facts, but that no amount of effort on the part of Lord Winterton could turn an original falsehood into a truth.

This polemic between the Soviet Embassy and a member of the British Government aroused universal attention in the heated atmosphere of the day. The Labour Party put down a question in Parliament. The Prime Minister himself had to reply. One can easily understand how unattractive this was for him, and how strenuously he tried to remove the blame from his Governmental colleague. Nevertheless, Chamberlain was obliged to repudiate Winterton's statement. We could feel some small satisfaction.

But it was small indeed. The great and truly important consideration which presented itself in all its magnitude to the Soviet State and the Soviet Government was Britain's position in the international arena. This could only arouse, and did of course arouse, profound concern and indignation. The notorious Four Power Pact had come into existence at Munich, its sharp edge turned against the U.S.S.R. And in the most base and repulsive form—a Four-Power Pact in which the unchallenged masters were the Fascist dictators, while the representatives of Britain and France were hurrying along in cowardly servility behind them. How characteristic, in fact, had been the behaviour of the British Government in the critical days of September. It had not once made an attempt even to consult the Government of the U.S.S.R. on the question of Czechoslovakia and of European peace. All the negotiations between Chamberlain and Mussolini, all Chamberlain's travels for meetings with the Fascist dictators, all his agreements with them, including that of Munich, were carried on behind the back of the Soviet Government, even without informing it of what was going on. The only time Halifax made contact with me about the events which had developed in September was in a conversation on September 29, that is, at a moment when Chamberlain was already in Munich and the fate of Czechoslovakia had already been settled. But what was the subject of this conversation? Britain's attitude on the question of Czechoslovakia? The prospects and lines of an agreement with Germany and Italy? Nothing of the kind. In his conversation Halifax wanted to explain to me why Britain and France had agreed to enter a conference with the Fascist dictators without the U.S.S.R. But Halifax's justification was worse than the most severe act of accusation against Chamberlain's policy. Here are the authentic words of Halifax, from his own record of our conversation:

'We all had to face facts, and one of these facts was, as he [i.e. I—I.M.] very well knew, that the heads of the German Government and of the Italian Government would not be willing in

present circumstances to sit in conference with Soviet representatives. It seemed to us vital, as I believed it would to him, that if
war was to be avoided, we must somehow or other get matters on to
a basis of negotiation. It was this conclusion that had led the Prime
Minister to make his appeal yesterday to Herr Hitler for a conference, to which, if Herr Hitler so desired, others could be invited.'[1]

This was a real certificate of poverty, issued to the British
Government by its own Foreign Secretary. For how in fact did
Halifax see the situation which had arisen? At the centre of all
things stands Hitler. To him is addressed the petition of the
Prime Minister of Great Britain to hold a conference, on him
depends likewise the composition of the conference. Chamberlain
himself can do nothing. He puts no conditions, he does not even
express any wishes. He simply and gratefully receives from the
hands of the Nazi dictator what the latter is pleased to throw him
from his table. It is difficult to imagine a picture of greater
humiliation for the head of the Government of one of the
greatest world Powers, whose possessions then could still be
found in all corners of the earth.

I did not hide from Halifax my sincere feelings, and quite
frankly told him what I thought of his words and of
Chamberlain's policy on international questions. I particularly
emphasized that the weakness displayed by the British Government in the events of 1938 not only did not put off but, on the
contrary, brought closer the peril of a second world war. Unfortunately, however, Halifax 'forgot' to reproduce these objections
of mine in his record of that conversation. But that is a not
infrequent occurrence in British diplomatic documents.

What conclusions did I draw—and could not help drawing—
from the painful experience of the Czechoslovak tragedy?

They were simple but not at all encouraging. I said to myself: 'This
is how Daladier's France carries out its obligations under treaties
which it has concluded! This is how Chamberlain's Britain observes
the requirements of the Covenant of the League of Nations!'

1. *Documents on British Foreign Policy*, *1919–1939*, Third Series, Vol.
II, pp. 623–4.

th:
th
th
re
pl
i
A

(

10

Chamberlain's sharp practice

IN NOVEMBER, 1938, when the excitement aroused by Munich had somewhat subsided, another serious event took place.

I have already said that on April 16, 1938, Chamberlain and Mussolini had signed an agreement for friendship and collaboration, but that, in an effort to calm British public opinion even to some extent, Chamberlain had promised that the treaty would not be ratified until the Italian troops had been withdrawn from Spain, in accordance with the plan of the Non-Intervention Committee. Such a plan, after prolonged discussions and arguments, was finally adopted on July 5, 1938. On the question of the evacuation of foreign combatants from Spain it provided that the number of evacuated combatants on the side which had fewest of them should be 10,000, while the side which had more was to evacuate a similar percentage of the total number of foreigners fighting on its side. Concretely this meant the following. In the summer of 1938 there were on the side of the Republican Government about 12,000 men, fighters in the famous International Brigades. Consequently 10,000 foreign combatants on the Republican side represented 80 per cent of their total. On the Franco side at that time, on the contrary, there were about 130,000 foreign combatants, among whom the Italians represented not less than 100,000. Consequently, in order to fulfil the conditions of the Committee's plan, Franco had to send home not less than 80,000 Italians. Naturally this did not suit Franco, and therefore in the autumn of 1938 he began a game of postponement. In this he was energetically supported by the Germans and Italians.

11

On the eve of 1939

As the New Year, 1939, opened I looked back over the results of my six years' work in London as Ambassador of the U.S.S.R. The review was not cheerful.

I had travelled here in 1932 with the very best intentions, and for six years, carrying out the instructions of the Soviet Government, had made very great efforts to improve relations between Britain and the U.S.S.R. This aim was likewise in keeping with my personal feelings and aspirations: from my boyhood I had cherished sympathy and respect for the British people, its high level of culture, its remarkable literature. I wanted so much to help in creating firm co-operation between the two countries. I was well aware that what the Soviet Government desired was also the desire of millions upon millions of Soviet people. Yet now, in the seventh year of my work in London, I was obliged to admit with bitterness that all these efforts were bearing less than modest fruits.

A Temporary Trade Agreement had been concluded (after a cruel struggle!) between the Soviet Union and Britain. For a year after that Anglo-Soviet relations were of a character that could be reckoned 'friendly'. I had succeeded in finding in Britain quite a number of wise, far-sighted and influential people among the ruling class, and in establishing good relations with them. All this was good and useful for the U.S.S.R., for Britain, for the cause of universal peace.

Nevertheless, power in this country remained firmly in the hands of the most reactionary elements of the Conservative Party. Chamberlain was Prime Minister and Lord Halifax was

94

Foreign Secretary, and it was the Cliveden set that defined the
main lines of the Government's official policy. That official
policy was directed sharply against the U.S.S.R. and the
principles of collective security; it was aimed at bringing about
conflict between Germany and the Soviet Union and was
sacrificing various countries and peoples to achieve its ends. The
examples of Austria, of Czechoslovakia, of Spain were particularly instructive.

And what did the future hold?

The European horizon was obscured by sinister clouds. To
avert a second world war would be possible only by the friendly
and joint efforts of the U.S.S.R., Great Britain, France and the
U.S.A. In practice it was collaboration between London and
Moscow that was particularly important. At one public meeting
during the winter of 1938–9 I said openly that the question of war
or peace depended in the long run on the character of relations
between Britain and the U.S.S.R. But what I had seen and
observed during my six years' work in London, what had
happened in Europe in 1938, made close co-operation unlikely
between the Powers who were not interested in launching war.
Least of all could one calculate that Chamberlain would accept
such co-operation.

Of course, even in such unfavourable circumstances I would
do all that was humanly possible for a *rapprochement* between
London and Moscow, for this was my duty as a Soviet
Ambassador, and in this lay the hope if not of averting at least of
somewhat postponing a second world war.

But all the same we entered 1939 with gloomy anticipations
and with a heavy burden of profound distrust of the then
Government of Great Britain, and above all of its head Neville
Chamberlain. Such was the psychological background on
which the events of that year of accursed memory wrote their
traces.

I have dwelt in such detail on my moods, thoughts and feelings
of that time, not at all because I attribute some particular personal
importance to them but only because they truthfully reflected

what the Soviet people, the Soviet State, the Soviet Government
were thinking and feeling. My psychology was a miniature
photographic reproduction of the psychology of the Soviet
whole, and only in that sense does it merit the attention of the
reader.

PART TWO

1939

ALL THAT has been set forth in the preceding pages represents only the prehistory of the tripartite negotiations for a pact of mutual assistance between the U.S.S.R., Great Britain and France. For this reason I have spoken of the events of 1932-8 briefly, omitting many details (often very characteristic), and drawing my picture in months or even years at a time. I now go on to my recollections of the tripartite negotiations themselves, the main theme of this book, and here I must alter the scale on which facts and events are depicted. Henceforth it is a question not of years or months but of weeks, days and in some cases even hours. That will make the picture more accurate, tangible and convincing.

I

The rape of Czechoslovakia
and Chamberlain's manœuvres

ON MARCH 10, 1939, Sir Samuel Hoare, Home Secretary and one of the most hardened Clivedenites, made a big speech in London. In it he depicted the European situation since Munich in the most optimistic colours. He declared that Britain and France did not want to attack anyone, underlined that Germany and Italy had repeatedly given assurances of their devotion to the cause of peace, and continued: *1 0 6 6 32*

'Suppose that political confidence could be restored to Europe; suppose that there was a five-year plan immensely greater than any five-year plan that this or that particular country has attempted in recent times, and that for a space of five years there were neither wars nor rumours of war. Suppose that the peoples of Europe were able to free themselves from a nightmare that haunts them and from an expenditure upon armaments that beggars them. Could we not then devote the almost incredible inventions and discoveries of our time to the creation of a golden age in which poverty could be reduced to insignificance, and the standard of living raised to heights that we have never been able to attempt before?

'Here indeed is the greatest opportunity that has ever been offered to the leaders of the world. Five men in Europe [Hoare had in mind the heads of Government in Britain, France, Germany, Italy and the U.S.S.R.—I.M.], if they worked with a singleness of purpose and a unity of action to this end, might in an incredibly short space of time transform the whole history of

the world. . . . Our own Prime Minister has shown his determination to work heart and soul to such an end. I cannot believe that
the other leaders of Europe will not join him in the high endeav-
our upon which he is engaged.'

When one now re-reads the speech of Sir Samuel Hoare it is
difficult to conceive of a more vivid example of hypocrisy,
stupidity and complete lack of understanding of what was really
going on in the world (though, of course, Halifax after Munich
had spoken of the coming of fifty years of peace in Europe!).
But even then, in March 1939, the more sober and thoughtful
politicians found Hoare's speech foolish, and even dangerous,
since it was calculated to lull the vigilance of wide circles of the
people and psychologically disarm them in face of the very great
danger of war. Real life very soon exposed the true value of that
gilded tinsel which the Home Secretary had so generously
distributed.

Exactly five days after his speech, on March 15, Hitler made
his lightning attack on Czechoslovakia, occupied Prague and
declared Bohemia and Moravia a German Protectorate, while
he transformed Slovakia into an 'independent state'. Europe
shuddered under the impact of a political earthquake. The
Munich Agreement was torn to shreds.

How did Chamberlain react?

On that same day, March 15, the Prime Minister had to make
a statement in the House of Commons on the seizure of Czechoslovakia. Of course, in words he was obliged to condemn Hitler's
behaviour, but he did not think it necessary to recommend any
practical action to Parliament. Chamberlain continued ob-
stinately to assert that he would as before strive for the return of
an atmosphere of mutual understanding and goodwill among all
the Powers, and for the settling of international disputes by
negotiation. Chamberlain also asserted that, in spite of all that had
happened, he thought his policy at Munich correct, and was
convinced that it enjoyed the support of world public opinion.

Chamberlain's attitude aroused a violent reaction, not only on
the part of the Labour and Liberal Opposition but even from

certain elements in the Conservative Party. In particular, Eden sharply criticized the foreign policy of the Government, and gave the warning that the annexation of Czechoslovakia would be followed by new acts of aggression on the part of the Fascist dictators. Eden vigorously demanded the setting up of an all-party Coalition Government with the task of effective resistance to aggression, which would for this purpose enter upon close co-operation with other peaceable States.[1]

The following day, March 16, the British press unanimously attacked Germany and declared openly that Hitler could not be trusted. *The Times* called the rape of Czechoslovakia a 'cruel and brutal act of repression'; the *Daily Telegraph* described it as a 'monstrous crime'; the *Daily Herald* called Hitler's aggression the 'postscript to Munich', and appealed to the country to organize resistance to the Fascist dictators jointly with France, the U.S.S.R. and the U.S.A.; the *Yorkshire Post*, a newspaper with which Eden was connected, declared that Nazi promises could not be regarded with the confidence displayed in them in recent times by the British Government. The other newspapers declared themselves in the same spirit.

It was clear that the widest social and political circles in Great Britain, in particular the masses of the workers, were profoundly indignant not only at Hitler's aggression but also at the activities of their own Government. In such a situation Chamberlain was obliged to manœuvre. He changed his attitude very quickly. As early as March 17, i.e. two days after his statement in Parliament, the Prime Minister made a big speech at a Conservative meeting in Birmingham. The 'soul' of Chamberlain, as subsequent events proved, had not changed in the least, but the whole tone of the speech was quite different from that of his words two days before. This time he expressed his regret for the excessive moderation he had shown in Parliament, explaining it by the inadequate information he had had at that moment about the events in Czechoslovakia. He strongly condemned Hitler's aggressive actions, and gave the pledge that Britain would resist to the last

1. *Parliamentary Debates. House of Commons*, Vol. 345, cols. 435–62.

extremity any attempts by Germany to establish domination of the world. But on the question of what must be done to avert such a menace the Prime Minister was very vague and even ambiguous. In particular, he did not fail to state that he was not ready to assume indefinite obligations which might have to be fulfilled in conditions which could not at present be foreseen. Translated into more simple terms this meant that Chamberlain was an opponent of the conclusion of pacts of mutual assistance of a more general character with other countries (he had, of course, in mind the U.S.S.R.).

Next day, March 18, Chamberlain undertook one more manœuvre, all the consequences of which, it must be supposed, he also did not at that time foresee. Immediately after Hitler had seized Czechoslovakia strong rumours spread through Europe (possibly inspired from Berlin) that the next victim would be Rumania. It was the Rumanian Minister in London, Tilea, who spread these rumours most actively. In the electrified atmosphere of those days such rumours were easily believed, because a new 'leap' in the direction of Rumania with its oilfields would be quite in keeping with the aggressive appetites of the Fuehrer. All admitted that it was possible and even probable. The rumours reached the British Government and caused it much alarm.

The result was that on the morning of March 18 Sir William Seeds, the British Ambassador in Moscow, visited the People's Commissar for Foreign Affairs and on the instructions of his Government asked him what the U.S.S.R. would do in the event of an attack by Hitler on Rumania. The same evening Litvinov, on the instructions of the Soviet Government, replied that the best means of combating the danger overhanging Rumania would be the immediate calling of a conference of representatives of Britain, France, the U.S.S.R., Turkey, Poland and Rumania. The Soviet Government considered, added Litvinov, that psychologically such a conference could be best of all summoned in Bucharest: but it was willing to agree to any other place found convenient by all participants in the conference.

In this way began the tripartite negotiations of 1939 between the U.S.S.R., Britain and France, negotiations destined to play such a great part in the events which directly preceded the outbreak of the second world war.

At this point it will be timely to dwell for a moment on the views with which the two sides entered upon the negotiations. The Soviet side was striving more than ever for the preservation of peace. It understood perfectly how close the peril of a second world war had come, and was ready to use any appropriate means to avert or at least postpone it. The Soviet side cherished no illusions. Recent experience had left behind only extreme distrust and irritation towards the British Government, and particularly towards Chamberlain personally; but the Soviet side considered that in the sphere of international relations policy must be governed by reason and not by emotion. Hence the Soviet side, even after all the disappointments of the preceding years, thought it essential to try to bring about co-operation with Britain and France for resistance to the aggressors. The representatives of the Soviet side still nourished a faint hope that possibly the tragedy of Czechoslovakia had opened the eyes even of the Clivedenites to the danger of appeasing Hitler, a danger which threatened Britain herself, and that in view of this the Chamberlain Government might at long last agree to effective co-operation with the U.S.S.R. in averting a second world war. And even if such a hope in the long run proved illusory, nevertheless it was necessary to try to come to an understanding with Chamberlain and Daladier. That was why the Soviet Government gave its reply with such phenomenal speed (the same day!) to the British Government's enquiry of March 18, and made a proposal which testified to its readiness to take really effective steps against the danger looming over Rumania.

The behaviour of the British side, that is, the Chamberlain Government, was quite different. As later events showed, the tragedy of Czechoslovakia had taught the Cliveden set absolutely nothing. The general line of policy of the Chamberlain Government had not altered in the least. This Government, as before, put its chief hopes upon the launching of a German-Soviet war, and therefore least of all did it want to quarrel with Hitler. Chamberlain (I mention him here and further on not only as a person but also the embodiment of the majority views in the Conservative Party) still maintained his policy of class hatred in respect of the U.S.S.R., and was so blinded by that passion that he did not see, and did not wish to see, that abyss which precisely at that time was beginning more and more visibly to open before Great Britain.[1] Hence followed his behaviour in the course of the 1939 negotiations. If the British Prime Minister had really been concerned for the maintenance of peace, as he repeatedly declared, he would gladly have seized upon the proposal made to him by the Soviet Union on March 18. And if this had happened the whole sequence of subsequent events would have taken another direction. It is possible, and even probable, that in such an event there would have been no second world war. But Chamberlain continued stubbornly to strike at one point, like a woodpecker: the prospect of a Soviet-German war. Therefore on March 18 he not only did not seize the hand outstretched to him by the U.S.S.R. but, on the contrary, began that systematic sabotage of all attempts at honest collaboration with the Soviet Government which ran like a red thread through the conduct of the negotiations by the British side to the very end. Chamberlain was so profoundly convinced of the infallibility of his political calculations, and of the inevitability of a German-Soviet conflict, that he did not even notice war creeping up to his own country much sooner than to the Soviet Union. However, more in detail of this later.

The sabotage of negotiations with the U.S.S.R. (one can find

1. Keith Feiling, Neville Chamberlain's biographer, quotes the following extract from Chamberlain's letter of March 26, 1939, to his sister: 'I must confess to the most profound distrust of Russia. I have no belief whatever in her ability to maintain an effective offensive, even if she wanted to. And I distrust her motives, which seem to me to have little connection with our ideas of liberty, and to be concerned only with getting everyone else by the ears' (*The Life of Neville Chamberlain*, 1946, p. 403).

It will be seen that our own distrust of Neville Chamberlain at that time was well founded.

no other name for it) began on March 18, 1939. The following morning I received a telegram from Moscow informing me of the conversations which had taken place between Seeds and Litvinov the day before. Remembering the tendentious 'subjectivity' of Sir Esmond Ovey during the Anglo-Soviet conflict over the Metropolitan-Vickers case in 1933, when the Ambassador had sent extremely inexact reports to London on his conversations with Litvinov, I decided this time, parallel with the Anglo-Soviet negotiations in Moscow, to inform Halifax of all that was going on there from my end as well. This would make it easier to anticipate any misinformation on the part of Seeds should he wish to follow Ovey's example. To be fair, however, I must say that throughout the tripartite negotiations we had no justification for suspecting Sir William of any act of bad faith.

And so, having received on the morning of the 19th the communication from Moscow about the Seeds-Litvinov talks, I at once asked for a meeting with Halifax, and repeated to him what Litvinov had said. Halifax thanked me for the information, and stated at once that the British Government had that morning already discussed the Soviet proposal for the immediate summoning of a Six-Power Conference, and had come to the conclusion that such a conference was undesirable.

I asked why.

Halifax's reply was very significant. The Foreign Secretary put forward two arguments: in the first place the British Government could not at present find a sufficiently responsible person to send to such a conference and, secondly, it was risky to call a conference without knowing how it would end.

I looked at Halifax with surprise, and did not conceal that these arguments seemed to me most unconvincing. In particular, I expressed the opinion that if the U.S.S.R., Britain and France were unanimous the conference could not end unsuccessfully. Halifax, however, did not agree with me, and I drew the only possible conclusion—that evidently he did not believe that unanimity between the U.S.S.R. on one side and Britain and France on the other was possible. This alone was very symptomatic.

In conclusion Halifax said that, fully realizing the necessity for urgent action, the British and French governments were now discussing another measure which might take the place of the Soviet proposal. But he evaded a more precise reply to my question as to what exactly was intended.[1]

Two days later, on March 21, this became known. The British and French put forward a scheme for the immediate publication of a declaration, signed by four Powers—Britain, France, the U.S.S.R. and Poland—to the effect that in the event of a new act of aggression the Powers concerned would immediately consult in order to discuss the measures which should be adopted.

The Soviet Government again replied very rapidly. On March 22 Litvinov informed Seeds, and on March 23 I informed Cadogan, Permanent Under-Secretary for Foreign Affairs, that although the U.S.S.R. considered this measure insufficiently effective, none the less it was ready to sign the declaration as soon as France and Poland did so. On the same day, March 23, Chamberlain stated in Parliament that he was an opponent of the setting up in Europe of blocs of Powers opposed to one another.[2] This still further reduced the value, low enough already, of the Four-Power declaration proposed by the British and French.

But even this politically anaemic declaration was not fated to see the light. Poland refused to sign it as a co-signatory with the U.S.S.R., and Chamberlain and Daladier did not think it necessary to exercise the necessary pressure on her. In conversation with me on March 23, Cadogan explained the behaviour of the Polish Government by its fear that such open association with the U.S.S.R. would make Germany angry.[3] I can allow that this motive might have played a certain part in the refusal of the Poles to sign the declaration, but the main reason lay elsewhere, of course. The main reason was the profound hostility of the then

1. *Documents on British Foreign Policy, 1919–1939*, Third Series, Vol. IV, p. 392.

2. *Parliamentary Debates. House of Commons*, Vol. 345, col. 1462.

3. *Documents on British Foreign Policy, 1919–1939*, Third Series, Vol. IV, p. 531.

Polish Government (the notorious 'Government of Colonels') towards the Soviet Union. This hostility, as we shall see further, knocked the last nail into the coffin of the tripartite negotiations of 1939.

Thus the draft Four-Power declaration had failed. What was now left for the Clivedenites to do? They would have most preferred to have done nothing at all. But this was difficult. The wave of public indignation aroused in Britain by the annexation of Czechoslovakia still stood very high. On March 22 Hitler had occupied Memel, and Mussolini pronounced a thunderous speech in support of his action. This still further increased the anti-Fascist mood in the country. Chamberlain had once again to resort to manœuvres capable of tranquillizing, at least to some extent, excited public opinion. So he thought of a device which was patent evidence of his complete helplessness.

On March 31 the Prime Minister unexpectedly invited me to come and see him at twelve noon. When I was in his study he handed me a sheet of paper, saying: 'Please read through this.'

I began rapidly to run through the typed sentences. They constituted an official statement by the British Government that, while consultations were now going on with other governments, and before those consultations were concluded, the British Government would come to the aid of Poland with all its resources if during that period there occurred 'any action which clearly threatened Polish independence and which the Polish Government accordingly considered it vital to resist with their national forces'. Britain required no reciprocity from Poland.

'I will be reading this statement today at 2 p.m. in the House of Commons,' said Chamberlain, when I had finished reading. 'I hope its contents will not arouse any objections on your side. Mr. Stalin in his recent speech at the Congress of your Party also promised the support of the Soviet Union to any country which became a victim of aggression and resisted the aggressor. . . . May I say in Parliament today that our guarantee to Poland meets with the approval of the Soviet Union?'

I was outraged by Chamberlain's unceremoniousness, but maintained my external calm and replied:

'I do not understand your request. Without any preliminary consultation with the Soviet Government, and quite independently, the British Government has decided to give a guarantee to Poland. I learn of this decision only now, two hours before its publication in the House of Commons. I have not the physical possibility in such a short time of making contact with my Government and learning its opinion of your declaration. How then can I authorize you to state that the Soviet Government approves the declaration? No, whatever its contents, I cannot on my own responsibility give you this authorization.'

Chamberlain expressed his regret at my reply, and we parted. The same day the Prime Minister informed Parliament of the Government's decision. The House approved it. In his explanatory statement Chamberlain did not venture to assert that the British guarantee to Poland had been approved by the Soviet Union, but nevertheless he said: 'I have no doubt that the principles on the basis of which we are acting meet with the understanding and sympathy of the Soviet Government.' The Prime Minister needed this hint in order to create the impression (possibly the general public would not be too inquisitive about the details) that the British Government was maintaining contact with the Soviet Government in order jointly to work out measures to resist Fascist aggression. The mass of the people were at that time demanding such a contact, and the closer it was the better.

At the same time France gave a similar guarantee to Poland.

Three days later Beck, Polish Foreign Minister and the effective leader of the 'Government of Colonels', arrived in London. During his three days' stay he carried on negotiations with Chamberlain and Halifax. As a result, the unilateral British guarantee to Poland was transformed into a bilateral one, so that in the event of 'any action' threatening British independence Poland would likewise come to the aid of Britain. In addition, it was decided to begin discussions for the conclusion of a formal pact of mutual assistance between the two countries. Anticipating a little, I will mention that these negotiations for various reasons dragged on and on, and the Anglo-Polish Pact of Mutual Assistance was signed in London only a few days before the outbreak of the second world war.

The British guarantee to Poland had been announced, a pact of mutual assistance with Poland had been promised, but there was no clarity as to what this meant in practice. On April 6, in conversation with Halifax, I asked whether the guarantee would be supported by military negotiations between the General Staffs of the two countries. The Foreign Secretary's reply was very characteristic:

'Conversations between the Staffs, certainly, are not excluded. It may well be that they will be found convenient. But so far nothing definite about this has been decided.'

To my further question as to what should be understood by the Premier's expression, in the course of his statement about the talks with Beck, that each side would come to the help of the other in the event of any threat, 'direct or indirect', to its independence, Halifax shrugged his shoulders and replied:

'Yes, this is undoubtedly a question on which it is vital to be clear, but the Polish Government and we will have further discussions about it.'[1]

It was obvious that the guarantee to Poland was still only a scrap of paper. Its future significance was vague and mysterious.

On April 7 Mussolini occupied Albania, once again by a lightning blow. There were stubborn rumours that he would not confine himself to this, and would also seize the Greek island of Corfu.

Panic broke out among the Clivedenites. During barely three weeks there had been three most undoubted acts of aggression: on March 15 against Czechoslovakia, on March 22 against Lithuania, and now on April 7 against Albania. Hitler and Mussolini, encouraged by the appeasers of Paris, London and Washington, had completely thrown off all restraint. Could it

1. *Documents on British Foreign Policy, 1919–1939*, Third Series, Vol. V, p. 53.

be that the Cliveden policy of conspiracy with the aggressors
against the U.S.S.R. had collapsed? Could it be that the opponents
of that policy would gain the upper hand? The Clivedenites could
not reconcile themselves to such a prospect.

And so the most feverish activity broke out in political circles
in London. The Prime Minister had just gone on holiday trout-
fishing in Scotland (he was a passionate angler), but he returned
immediately to the capital. There was an extraordinary meeting
of the Cabinet with the leaders of the Liberal and Labour
Opposition in attendance. A special meeting of the Committee of
Imperial Defence was held. British naval forces began to
concentrate at Gibraltar and Malta. Halifax made a protest to the
Italian *chargé d'affaires* against the seizure of Albania, and tried
to frighten him with the 'strong feelings' which Mussolini's
aggression had aroused in Britain. Continuous consultations went
on between London and Paris as to what was to be done.

The alarm spread to the Continent. France, Belgium and
Holland called up certain classes of reservists, and the mouths
of the Scheldt and Meuse were mined. Italy increased her armed
forces to 1,200,000 men. It was stated in Washington that the
actions of the aggressors had destroyed confidence on the
international field, and that this was a threat to the security of
the U.S.A.

In such a situation the British Government was compelled to
do something—and something, moreover, which would appear
as a display of speed, resolution and energy. As a result,
Chamberlain on April 13 stated in Parliament that Britain was
giving a unilateral guarantee to Rumania and Greece, like that
which on March 31 had been given to Poland. On the same day
France made a similar statement.

Only now, when Britain had hastily assumed the obligation to
defend the independence of the three countries named, did
Chamberlain think it timely to remember the U.S.S.R. On April 14
the British Government made an official proposal to the Soviet
Government that it should give Poland and Rumania the same
kind of unilateral guarantee that Britain and France had given

Poland on March 31, and Rumania and Greece on April 13. On its part, the French Government proposed a draft joint declaration by the U.S.S.R. and France, based on the principle of mutual obligations.

On the same day, April 14, Roosevelt addressed an appeal to Germany and Italy to keep the peace and abstain from aggression. In Berlin this appeal was met with coarse abuse, while Mussolini replied that that was just what he was concerned with—how to strengthen peace and co-operation among the peoples! In Britain and France Roosevelt's appeal met with warm support. The U.S.S.R. also was sympathetic, and M. I. Kalinin (then President of the Presidium of the Supreme Soviet) sent Roosevelt a telegram in this sense. But the practical significance of the American President's action was, at the very best, modest.

During the years which have passed since these events many attempts have been made to give a satisfactory explanation of the policy of unilateral 'guarantees' which the British Government adopted in March and April, 1939. This was not easy, because from the standpoint of common sense, which the British so respect, Chamberlain's behaviour in those critical weeks resembled lunacy. I remember that immediately after the guarantee to Rumania and Greece had been proclaimed Lloyd George said to me:

'You know I have never had a high opinion of Chamberlain, but what he is doing now is breaking all records for stupidity. . . . We are giving guarantees to Poland and Rumania, but what can we do for them if they are attacked by Hitler? Practically nothing. Geographically these two countries are so situated that we cannot reach them. Even arms and munitions can only be supplied to them through Soviet territory. The key to their salvation lies in your hands. Without Russia nothing can be done. . . . So first of all there should have been an agreement with Moscow. But what does Chamberlain do? Without coming to any agreement with the Soviet Union, and in fact behind its back, he distributes "guarantees" right and left to countries in Eastern Europe. What crying folly! What a disgrace for British diplomacy!'

There was much truth in Lloyd George's words. It was no secret to any politically literate person that even if Britain and France wanted conscientiously to perform the obligations they had assumed, their help to Poland and Rumania could not be particularly effective. At best it could take only the form of operations holding down part of the German Army to the Franco-German frontier, the organization of a naval blockade of Germany, and British and French air raids on her. In Hitler's hands there would remain in all circumstances sufficient armed forces rapidly to overthrow the Polish and Rumanian armies. What then was the real value of the Anglo-French guarantees? And what would have been the situation of Britain and France if, these guarantees being tested in practice, their military insignificance had been revealed?

Chamberlain's behaviour was in complete contradiction to the usual caution and prudence of British foreign policy. It looked like a break with the diplomatic traditions of the past, and there was a moment when it even seemed to me that it might lead, against the will of Chamberlain himself, to great consequences favourable to the cause of peace. But the power of the Cliveden set and its thick-wittedness in the sphere of foreign policy soon banished such ideas from my mind. It very soon became clear that Chamberlain was incorrigible, and that his main political aim of provoking a conflict between Germany and the U.S.S.R. remained in full force. How then could one nevertheless explain the appearance of his policy of guarantees?

When today, many years later, I sum up all that I saw and observed in 1939, and all that I have since learned from the books, memoirs and documents published since the war, I am inclined to give this reply:

In March and April, 1939, Chamberlain was as faithful as ever to his political line. For its sake he put up easily with the destruction of Austria, Czechoslovakia, Memel, Albania—which had already taken place—and would no less easily have put up with the destruction of Rumania and Poland—which might yet take place. An extremely narrow-minded and stubborn man, as we know, Chamberlain moved directly to his objective, without looking to right or to left. Moreover he had behind him the powerful support of the Cliveden set of which he was at that time the leader.

But the Prime Minister was overtaken by a tempest of events over which he had no control. The insolent acts of Fascist aggression caused profound alarm in France and in a number of small countries (Belgium, Holland, Switzerland, Denmark, Norway, Sweden and others) which had political or economic ties with Great Britain. These countries, independently of whether they had any treaties with Britain, spontaneously gravitated to London and were now seeking its protection against the peril which had suddenly arisen.

The same impudent acts of Fascist aggression aroused in Britain herself a great wave of public indignation and concern. People of the most varied views and social condition (including considerable circles of the bourgeoisie) were involuntarily asking themselves: Where was Britain going? Where was Europe going? Could the world really be moving towards Fascist dictatorship? Was the Government's policy correct when it was only increasing the appetite of Hitler and Mussolini for aggression? And many, very many, people (the great mass of the Labour Movement in particular) replied: 'No, the policy of the Government is wrong and even criminal. There are sufficient forces in the world to crush the Fascist aggressors, and at all events to stop their aggression. What is needed is to combine and organize those forces. And in the first place it is essential to bring into being, together with the Soviet Union, a mighty coalition for peace and resistance to the Fascist dictators.'

To these external and internal forces which were counteracting Chamberlain's general line there was also added powerful pressure from the U.S.S.R., which was demanding resolute struggle against the German-Italian aggressors as the only way to prevent a second world war.

All these influences, intertwined and interacting, were building up in Britain such a political atmosphere that the Cliveden set

H

was unwillingly having to face the question of whether it would be able to remain in power? In order to parry the danger of the forced resignation of Chamberlain the Cliveden set had to manœuvre. As Sir Samuel Hoare said one Saturday at Lady Astor's house it was necessary to throw the dog a bone to make it stop barking, if only for a time. Actions had to be urgent and hasty. There was no time to think out all the possible consequences of the measures adopted. The best specialists in foreign policy, like Vansittart or Eden, had been eliminated. Halifax, himself one of the members of the Cliveden set, willingly drifted along the stream, leaving the Prime Minister full freedom of action. The whole foreign policy of Great Britain in those days was being made by Chamberlain, together with his evil genius Sir Horace Wilson. As a consequence, the British Government's actions in March and April, 1939, often bore an accidental, hasty and near-sighted character. If there was in them any element of statesmanship in the main it amounted to the two following considerations:

(a) By giving 'guarantees' to Poland, Rumania and Greece the internal opposition was to be pacified and the Cliveden set preserved in office.

(b) A certain psychological pressure would be exercised on Hitler and Mussolini, and new acts of aggression by them disadvantageous for Britain could be delayed, in the hope that in the meantime some change in the international situation would enable the Clivedenites to return to the open and consistent pursuit of their general line.

The first consideration, of course, was the principal one: but the second, too, was taken seriously, since thereby the Clivedenites were gaining time in the hope of avoiding any necessity to accept co-operation with the U.S.S.R.

Moreover, as was shown by the suggestion that the Soviet Government should give a unilateral guarantee to Poland and Rumania, the Clivedenites cherished the quite unfounded hope that, in one way or another, if not on the swings then on the roundabouts, they would force the Soviet Union to serve their own interests without assuming any obligations whatever in relation to our country.

And finally, if all the rest did not produce the desired result, the Clivedenites had in reserve one more 'way out': to betray Poland, Rumania and Greece, as they had just betrayed Czechoslovakia, Austria and Spain.

Naturally, the Clivedenite policy, so zealously applied by Chamberlain, was a policy of blindness and stupidity. The subsequent course of events demonstrated this completely. But that always happens when, at a turning point in history, power is in the hands of the representatives of reaction and obscurantism.

2

The U.S.S.R. proposes a pact
of mutual assistance

THE British Government's suggestion that the Soviet Union should give a unilateral guarantee to Poland and Rumania brought the Soviet Government face to face with the question of what the really effective measures would be to prevent further Fascist aggressions.

What Chamberlain was trying to get us to do was unacceptable to the Soviet Government for two reasons—it could not prevent the outbreak of a second world war, which was our main aim; and it put the U.S.S.R. in an unequal position compared with Britain and France, greatly increasing the danger of an attack by Germany on our country.

In fact, Hitler and Mussolini properly understood only one argument—force. Consequently, to avert further Fascist aggressions, and the inevitable consequence of a second world war, it was necessary to bring into being such a powerful defensive coalition that Hitler and Mussolini would lose the inclination to test its strength. We considered that Britain, France and the U.S.S.R., taken together, disposed of the necessary strength, but if this was really to stay the hand of the Fascist dictators there must be no doubt that this strength would really fall upon them at any new attempted aggression. And this in its turn required that the combination of these three Powers should be visible, indubitable, that its sphere of operation should include the whole of Europe and not separate corners of the Continent, and that the terms of the alliance should provide the simplest and most automatic system of sanctions possible against the aggressor.

But the British proposal did not answer such requirements at all. In the first place it did not set up any common combination of the U.S.S.R., Britain and France to combat aggression in Europe; it confined itself to joint operations by the three Powers only in the event of an attack by Germany on Poland and Rumania. Thus the British proposal could not prevent war at all: it might only 'canalize' aggression in those directions which were not protected by guarantees—and particularly in such an important direction for the U.S.S.R. as the Baltic States.

Furthermore, the British proposal did not provide for any military convention between the three Great Powers establishing precisely the dimensions, dates, conditions, etc., of armed assistance which they would afford one another and the victim of aggression. Yet this was of first-class importance. The Soviet Union already had an extremely unpleasant experience with France in this respect. In May, 1935, as has already been mentioned, a Pact of Mutual Assistance had been concluded between the U.S.S.R. and France, but the drafting and signature of a supporting military convention had been postponed until later. The French Governments which rapidly succeeded one another thereafter systematically sabotaged the conclusion of such a convention, however, and in 1939 it still did not exist. Naturally the absence in the British proposal of any hint of the possible conclusion of a military convention was regarded by the Soviet Government as a very serious defect. Any agreement to combat the aggressors had to have sharp teeth. Without such teeth it became a sword of cardboard, which could be waved but which could not strike a blow.

When guarantees were so indefinite, there were bound to be differences among participants in the agreement in interpreting the obligations they had assumed, and difficulties in working out a common strategy and tactics, delay in action and many other loose ends were inevitable. In the long run the British proposition could not promote that concentration of forces on the side of the peace-loving powers which alone could restrain the Fascist dictators from new acts of aggression. And still less could it assure rapidity and unity of punitive operations by Britain, France and the U.S.S.R. against those who might wish to launch a second world war.

But the British proposal was not only useless for averting a new world slaughter: it was also insulting for the U.S.S.R. since it put the latter in an unequal position compared with Britain and France. The Soviet Government was interested here, of course, not in the legal but in the factual state of affairs. The factual situation was that Britain, France and Poland were bound by agreements for mutual assistance, and in the event of an attack by Germany on any one of them the other two Powers had immediately to come to its assistance with all their resources, including their armed forces. The Soviet Union, on the other hand, had a pact of mutual assistance only with France. Neither Britain nor Poland was obliged to assist it in the event of a German attack. Yet the granting by the Soviet Union of a guarantee to Poland and Rumania was bound beyond question to worsen its relation with Germany, and increase the peril of Hitlerite aggression against the Soviet Union, in particular through the Baltic States. The result was obvious inequality between the U.S.S.R. on the one hand and Britain and France on the other in such an important respect as national and State security. This was of the highest importance.

Such were the main considerations which obliged the Soviet Government to reject the British proposal. But it did not stop at that. Although the experience of Czechoslovakia and Spain had greatly undermined its belief that Britain and France were ready conscientiously to fulfil obligations they had assumed, although their behaviour over the seizure of Memel and Albania by the Fascist Powers augured nothing of promise, nevertheless the Soviet Government did not think itself entitled to wash its hands of them. The moment was too serious, the peril of a second world war too great, to allow even quite legitimate emotion to induce it to throw aside even the tiniest chance of preserving the world from a new and terrible catastrophe. At this fateful hour the Soviet Government decided to follow only the dictates of common sense, and to make one more attempt to come to an agreement with Britain and France for joint action against the Fascist aggressors. But it had to be a really serious attempt, putting forward serious proposals for the adoption of serious means of reaching the objective—to avert a second world war.

Taking into account both the British and the French attitudes, the Government of the U.S.S.R. on April 17, 1939—that is, three days after the British Government had proposed that we should give a unilateral guarantee to Poland and Rumania—put forward its own proposition. Essentially it amounted to three basic points:

1. The conclusion of a triple pact of mutual assistance between the U.S.S.R., Great Britain and France.

2. The conclusion of a military convention to reinforce this pact.

3. The provision of a guarantee of independence for all the States bordering on the U.S.S.R., from the Baltic to the Black Sea.

In handing our counter-proposition to Halifax, I said:

'If Britain and France really want to resist the aggressors seriously, and to avert a second world war, they will be bound to accept the Soviet proposals. But if they don't accept them . . .' There I made a gesture, the sense of which it was not difficult to understand.

Halifax began to assure me of the utter seriousness of British and French intentions, but silently I said to myself: 'Facts will show.'

At the same time as he sent me our counter-propositions M. M. Litvinov recalled me to Moscow to take part in a Government discussion on the question of the triple pact of mutual assistance and the prospects of its conclusion. On April 19 I left London, and returned nine days later. The sight of Nazi Germany with its swastikas and goose-stepping soldiery was repulsive to me, and I decided to travel by a roundabout route. A plane took me from London to Stockholm, and from there to Helsinki, where I took the train to Leningrad and so to Moscow. On the way I spent the night at Stockholm, and had a long and interesting conversation on current political subjects with my old friend of emigrant days, Alexandra Mihailovna Kollontay, then Minister of the U.S.S.R. in Sweden.

'Can Chamberlain really not understand that his policy is leading Britain straight to disaster?' Alexandra Mihailovna asked me in surprise.

I described to her in detail the situation which had arisen in London, and summed up at the end:

'Class hatred can so blind people that they cease to see the most ordinary things. I am being shown this just now by the example of Chamberlain and the whole Cliveden set. Of course, history will punish them severely, but unfortunately that will probably be after the guns have begun to fire.'

In Moscow I attended the Government conference, at which the question of a triple pact was examined in great detail. I had to give the fullest possible information and explanation about the state of public feeling in Britain, the relationship of forces between the supporters and opponents of a pact, the position of the Government as a whole and of its individual members in respect of the pact, the immediate political prospects in the British Isles and many other questions bound up in one way or another with the probable destiny of the Soviet counter-proposals.

When informing the Government, I tried to be honest and objective to the very limit. I have always considered that an Ambassador must frankly tell his Government the truth, and must create no illusions in its midst, either optimistic or pessimistic. Basing itself on the information of its Ambassador, the Government may enter upon this or that practical line of policy, and if the Ambassador's information has been artificially coloured in too rosy or too darkened a hue the Government may find itself in a difficult or embarrassing situation. Observing this principle strictly, I have sometimes had some unpleasant experiences, but nevertheless continued to do what I thought right. At that well-remembered conference in the Kremlin, I repeat, I told the truth and only the truth—and the picture in consequence was not a very consoling one. None the less, the Government decided to continue the negotiations, and to make every possible effort to persuade the British and the French to change their attitude. For both at this Conference and in private conversations with members of the Government whom I knew, I felt dominating everything, all the way through, one idea: 'At all costs a new world war must be avoided. An agreement must be reached as soon as possible with Britain and France.'

I returned the same way, but from Stockholm I flew not directly to London but to Paris, in order to get to know better the feelings of the French Government in relation to the pact. Our Ambassador in France, Yakov Zaharovich Suritz, a most cultivated man with a wide political horizon, willingly acquainted me with the situation in Paris in all its detail.

'With all his defects, and he has plenty,' concluded Suritz, 'Daladier would nevertheless meet our counter-proposals more favourably than Chamberlain. Moreover, France has already, of course, its Pact of Mutual Assistance with the U.S.S.R.—at any rate, on paper. . . . At this very moment, for example, the French Government is pressing the British to accept our proposals for a triple pact, made on April 17, as a basis. Léger [the secretary-general of the French Ministry for Foreign Affairs] has even drawn up a counter-draft to present to the Soviet Government. It is not so comprehensive as ours, but is on the same basis. But London doesn't want to accept it, and continues to maintain its proposal for a unilateral guarantee by the U.S.S.R. to Poland and Rumania which it made on April 14. I don't know how the Anglo-French argument will end, but I am pessimistic.'

Suritz waved his hand hopelessly, and went on: 'The whole trouble is that France nowadays has no independent foreign policy, and everything depends on London. France nowadays is a Great Power of the second rank, which is still reckoned a Great Power by tradition more than anything else. And the strange thing is that the French have somehow become reconciled to it, and plod along at Britain's tail. In the Anglo-French bloc they regard themselves as Power No. 2, and are not indignant. . . .'

'Well, and how are the Americans behaving here?' I asked.

'The Americans?' said Suritz. 'I think the name of their Ambassador here—William Bullitt—tells you the whole story.'

There went through my mind a chain of recollections—Bullitt the representative of President Wilson, who in March, 1919, had come to Moscow with the offer of peace; Bullitt the active participant in Soviet-American negotiations in Washington in 1933 for mutual diplomatic recognition; Bullitt the first American Ambassador in Moscow, who became famous for his extravagant diplomatic receptions[1] and (what was much more important) who tried under cover of external friendliness to dictate to the Soviet Government; Bullitt, who had changed from 'friend' to enemy after getting a rebuff from the Soviet Government. . . . And now this same Bullitt represented the U.S.A. in France.

Suritz went on: 'Bullitt is very interested in the course of the negotiations, gives his advice, sometimes reads them lectures based on his supposed knowledge of the U.S.S.R. and its Government. Of course, his opinion counts for a great deal with Daladier and Bonnet. After all, he supported them energetically in the days of Munich, and even met Daladier with a bouquet of flowers when the Premier returned home after the Munich betrayal.'

Later on, when the negotiations had developed, Bullitt more than once tried to obstruct them with his 'advice' to Bonnet and Daladier. This, of course, only intensified the sabotage, with the spirit of which the British and French governments were already well saturated even without his help.

On April 29, the day following my return from Moscow, I visited Halifax. Still full of my fresh Moscow impressions, I long

1. Once, for example, Bullitt arranged in his Embassy a diplomatic reception which was more like some witches' Sabbath. During this reception it was not only a case of rivers of champagne flowing and various dishes in homeric dimension, but the building itself was transformed into something recalling a menagerie: birds flew about the rooms, goats ran about among the tables, while a live bear stood growling angrily in a 'place of honour' in the corner, among the plants. Of course, such a reception was quite an exceptional 'sensation' in Hollywood style—but it added nothing to the standing of the American Ambassador.

and warmly demonstrated to the Foreign Secretary the importance of concluding a triple pact of mutual assistance as rapidly as
possible, and assured him insistently of the most sincere desire of
the Soviet Government to co-operate with Britain and France in
resisting aggression. Halifax listened to me with a sceptical smile,
and when I asked him whether the British Government accepted
our counter-proposals he replied very vaguely that it had not yet
completed its consultations with France. This had the effect on
me of a bucket of cold water. Then he talked of other current
affairs—Britain's negotiations with Rumania, the various sugges-
tions for an Anglo-Turkish agreement and so on. I left the
Foreign Office very irritated with the obstinate blindness of the
Cliveden set.

During my visit to Moscow two events had taken place which
were clear evidence that the aggressors had taken the bit between
their teeth, and were tearing along at full speed to their criminal
objective: on April 28 Hitler had simultaneously torn up his Pact
of Non-Aggression with Poland and the Anglo-German Naval
Aggreement of 1935. But the Clivedenites did not see, or did not
want to see, these threatening signs of the times, and were wilfully
continuing their fatal progress towards the precipice. How
characteristic, for example, was the following fact which also
occurred during my absence from London. Immediately after the
annexation of Czechoslovakia the British Government had recalled Nevile Henderson, its Ambassador in Berlin, 'for consultations'—a symbolic gesture to show its dissatisfaction. But now,
on April 24, the British Government had permitted Henderson to
return to Berlin. This was also a symbolic gesture, but in the
directly opposite sense.

On May 3 Litvinov was relieved of his post as People's
Commissar for Foreign Affairs, and V. M. Molotov was appointed
in his place. This aroused a great sensation in Europe at the time,
and was interpreted as a change in the foreign policy of the
U.S.S.R.

Three days later, on May 6, Halifax asked me to come and see
him. Telling me that Britain had not yet concluded its consultations

with other capitals about the Soviet proposal for a pact of mutual assistance, he put the question direct: what did the changes in personnel which had just taken place in Moscow signify?

'Before communicating our reply to the Soviet proposal,' said Halifax, 'I should like to know whether these changes also signify a change of policy? Do the proposals made by you still hold the field?'[1]

'Contrary to what often happens in the West,' I said, 'individual Ministers in the Soviet Union do not conduct their own policy. Every Minister puts into effect the general policy of the Government as a whole. Therefore, although M. M. Litvinov has resigned as People's Commissar for Foreign Affairs, the foreign policy of the Soviet Union remains the same. Consequently the proposals we made on April 17 remain in force.'

On May 8, after three weeks of consultation and meditation, the British Government at length handed us its reply—which was also the reply of France—to our proposals for a triple pact of mutual assistance. But what kind of a reply was it? The British Government repeated in a slightly modified form its previous proposals of April 14, i.e. it continued to press for a unilateral guarantee to Poland and Rumania by the Soviet Union. Evidently the resistance of France had been of no avail, and the pessimistic anticipations of Suritz had been justified.

It was clear that the Clivedenites, and particularly Chamberlain, were continuing to put their money on a conflict between Germany and the U.S.S.R., and therefore did not want to quarrel with Hitler. It was also clear that all the negotiations for co-operation between Britain and the U.S.S.R. to resist the aggressors were merely a hypocritical manœuvre by the British Government to deceive its own people, a smoke-screen to gain time for the purpose of applying the same general line of the Prime Minister. Not surprisingly, the Soviet Government reacted to the British reply with firmness and resolution. On May 15 Seeds was handed a written statement in Moscow, saying in black and white that the

1. *Documents on British Foreign Policy, 1919–1939*, Third Series, Vol. V, p. 453.

granting of a unilateral guarantee to Poland and Rumania was unacceptable for the Soviet Government, and that the only real and genuinely effective form of resistance to aggression was a triple pact of mutual assistance on the basis of the conditions set forth in the Soviet proposals of April 17. The whole tone of our reply was such that the British (and the French) were faced with a choice of either a pact of mutual assistance or the collapse of the negotiations.

There was an impasse—all the more strange because at that very time Britain and France concluded a Treaty of Mutual Assistance with Turkey. Excitement began to rise in the press and in political circles in London. The clouds on the international horizon were growing ever darker. Encouraged by the behaviour of Chamberlain and Daladier, Hitler was becoming more and more unbridled. Now he opened a furious campaign over Danzig, and demanded that Poland should return the city to Germany and give the latter freedom of transit across the Polish Corridor. The Polish Government rejected these claims. The atmosphere in Polish-German relations was growing more tense, and any day one might expect an explosion. Yet, in spite of all this, Chamberlain would not hear of accepting the Soviet proposals for a triple pact of mutual assistance. It is not surprising that all the more intelligent among the British politicians (not to speak of the great mass of the people) were extremely worried, and were looking for ways of exercising pressure on the Government.

On May 18 Churchill telephoned to me.

'Tomorrow,' he said, 'there will be a foreign policy debate in Parliament. I intend to speak, and to draw attention to the unsatisfactory way the negotiations with Russia are being carried on. . . . But before speaking on this subject in public I would like to know from you what exactly are the Soviet Government's proposals which Chamberlain doesn't want to accept? There are many rumours going about.'

I answered Churchill's question in detail on the spot, by telephone. He listened very attentively, and when I had finished said with surprise:

'I don't understand what Chamberlain has found unsatisfactory in your proposals. I should think that they are all acceptable.'

'You know better how to interpret the Prime Minister's conduct,' I replied to Churchill with a laugh.

The next day, May 19, there did in fact develop a big debate on British foreign policy in the House of Commons. Churchill, as he had promised, made a big speech in which, among other things, he said the following:

'Undoubtedly the proposals put forward by the Russian Government contemplate a triple alliance against aggression between England, France and Russia, which alliance may extend its benefits to other countries if and when those benefits are desired. The alliance is solely for the purpose of resisting further acts of aggression and of protecting the victims of aggression. I cannot see what is wrong with that. . . . It is said: "Can you trust the Russian Soviet Government?" I suppose in Moscow they say: "Can we trust Chamberlain?" . . . In such questions one must be guided not by feelings but by an analysis of the interests involved. Personally I believe that the important and vital interests of Russia dictate to her co-operation with Britain and France in preventing further acts of aggression.'

After touching on the assertions of the Clivedenites that a triple pact was impossible because, forsooth, Poland, Rumania and the Baltic States were afraid of being guaranteed by an alliance in which the U.S.S.R. was included, Churchill ridiculed these arguments and added, addressing himself to members of the Government:

'If you are ready to be an ally of Russia in time of war . . . if you are ready to join hands with Russia in the defence of Poland, which you have guaranteed, and of Rumania, why should you shrink from becoming the ally of Russia now, when you may by that very fact prevent the outbreak of war?'

No less firmly did Lloyd George speak at the same sitting against the Government. Referring to the armament of Germany and Italy, he said:

'They are not preparing for defence. . . . They are not preparing themselves against attack from either France, Britain or Russia. That has never been threatened. . . . They are preparing for some contemplated offensive scheme against someone or other in whom we are interested. . . . The main military purpose and scheme of the dictators is to produce quick results, to avoid a prolonged war. A prolonged war never suits dictators.'

And in order not to permit a quick victory of the dictators Lloyd George thought it extremely necessary to bring into being as quickly as possible a triple agreement against them.

'Without the help of Russia it will be impossible to fulfil our obligations to Poland and Rumania,' said Lloyd George. The U.S.S.R. possessed the best air force in the world and extremely powerful tank forces. Why had the Government still not concluded a pact of mutual assistance with the U.S.S.R.? Evidently because it did not trust the Soviet Government. 'But has not Russia the grounds for not trusting us?' exclaimed Lloyd George. 'Since 1930 we have violated all the pacts we have signed bearing on a situation like the present.' In conclusion Lloyd George demanded that the Government should urgently complete the tripartite negotiations.

Eden also spoke warmly in favour of the building of a 'peace front' as rapidly as possible, and as a first step in this direction urged the immediate conclusion of a triple alliance between Britain, France and the U.S.S.R. on the basis of complete reciprocity and equality.[1]

The firm attitude of the U.S.S.R., on the one hand, and the Parliamentary debate on May 19, on the other, convinced Chamberlain that he needed to make a new hypocritical manœuvre. Otherwise the Government might fall between two stools. And Chamberlain carried out this manœuvre, but on this occasion in Geneva.

On May 22 the usual session of the Council of the League of Nations opened there. It was the turn for a representative of the U.S.S.R. to take the chair. The Soviet Government appointed me

1. *Parliamentary Debates. House of Commons*, Vol. 347, Cols. 1810–1960.

for this duty; and on May 20 I left London for Switzerland. I spent several hours in Paris on the way, and Suritz told me that the French Government had lately been expressing great dissatisfaction with the tardiness and obstinacy of the British in the negotiations with the U.S.S.R. Even Bonnet, then the French Foreign Minister and long an enemy of Moscow, thought that a critical situation had been reached and that an agreement should be concluded with the Soviet Government as soon as possible.

Halifax and Bonnet were also going to Geneva, and I had the prospect of meeting them daily at the Council table for a whole week. While still in London, Halifax had kindly warned me that he hoped to continue negotiations with myself in Switzerland. In fact, we had a meeting at Geneva on the morning of May 22, and had a long, and in a certain sense a 'decisive, conversation about the pact.

Halifax began by asking me to explain why the Soviet Government was rejecting the British proposal of May 8 (i.e. the slightly touched-up original proposal that the Soviet Union should give a unilateral guarantee to Poland and Rumania).

I replied that we were rejecting the British proposal for two main reasons: (a) we were striving to prevent war altogether, which was possible only with the help of a triple pact of mutual assistance, whereas the British proposal completely ignored this most important aspect; and (b) the British proposal put the U.S.S.R. in an unequal position compared with Britain and France, to which we could not in any way agree. And I briefly explained where we saw this inequality (I have already discussed this above).

Halifax began to argue that there was little probability of an attack by Germany on the U.S.S.R. through the Baltic States, and that even if such an attack did take place Poland and Rumania would also without doubt be drawn in, and in that event the Anglo-French guarantees to these two States would enter into force. In this way Britain and France would in practice come to the aid of the U.S.S.R.

I did not agree with Halifax, and said that the Anglo-French guarantees to Poland and Rumania did not impress me either.

'Imagine such a case,' I continued. 'Germany by terrorism, or bribery, or combining the tactics of carrot and lash, induces Poland and Rumania to enter into an alliance with her against the U.S.S.R., or at least allow Germany transit for her troops through their territory. In that event the British and French guarantees do not operate, because they are valid only on the condition that Poland and Rumania themselves are offering resistance to Germany. Consequently in such a hypothetical case, which is by no means improbable, the U.S.S.R. would have to fight Germany single-handed, without receiving any help from the Western Powers.' Halifax tried to parry my arguments by pointing out that France and the U.S.S.R. have a Pact of Mutual Assistance.

'Quite true,' I replied. 'But there is no such pact between Britain and the U.S.S.R., and that is of very great importance.'

Then Halifax suggested: 'Perhaps we could add an article to our proposals binding the States which have a common frontier with the U.S.S.R. not to allow the transit of German troops through their territory, or German bases to be built with the object of attacking your country?'

I expressed the opinion that the border States were hardly likely to agree to accept such an obligation, and even if they did agree would be simply unable to observe it. All these complicated and tortuous combinations, which the British side had spent so many efforts in working out, were of a half-hearted and amateur character. They decided nothing. The only genuinely effective way to resist aggression was the triple pact of mutual assistance being proposed by the Soviet Government.

Then all of a sudden Halifax took it into his head to try to frighten me. Such a pact might arouse Hitler to fury, he would begin to shout about 'encirclement' of Germany, this would unite the whole German people around him, and he would launch a war. In this way we would ourselves provoke precisely what we wanted to avert by our actions.

I retorted that Halifax evidently did not understand very well

I

the psychology of men like Hitler. In his own way he was not at all a fool. He would never engage in a war if he thought he might lose it. Even our present negotiations were forcing him to display a certain care: so far, for example, he had not attacked Poland. But if a triple pact of mutual assistance were concluded Hitler would be obliged to retreat. People like him recognized only one argument—force. The Soviet Government knew this well from its experience with Japan. And a triple pact of mutual assistance would bring into being such a concentration of power on the side of the forces of peace that there would be nothing left for the aggressors but to quieten down.

In conclusion Halifax asked whether the Soviet Government was ready to provide in any agreement for a triple pact of mutual assistance that there should be guarantees of security not only for the small East European States, but also for those in the West (Halifax gave me to understand that he had in mind Belgium, Holland and Switzerland).

I replied that I could not say anything about this at the moment, on behalf of the Soviet Government, since such a problem had not been raised or discussed up to the present: but I thought it could be examined, and it did not seem to me very difficult to solve.

Our conversation lasted an hour and a half, and when I was leaving it seemed to me to have made a considerable impression on the Foreign Secretary. In any case I had given him quite clearly to understand that in order to achieve agreement the Soviet Government could make concessions on secondary questions, but would accept no compromise on the basic three points which have been mentioned earlier (a triple pact of mutual assistance, a military convention, guarantees of security for all the small countries from the Baltic to the Black Sea).

Today, reading the documents published by the British Foreign Office, I see that my impression at the time was justified. Halifax concludes his record of the conversation with me on May 22 with the following words:

'I am afraid I was unable in the course of the long conversation to shake M. Maisky at all on his main points of insistence on a triple mutual guarantee against direct aggression. . . . I think the choice before us is disagreeably plain, i.e. break down of negotiations or agreement on lines of paragraph 4, telegram No. 165 to Warsaw' (i.e. a triple pact of mutual assistance—I.M.).

On the same day, May 22, I had a conversation on the same basic theme with Bonnet. The French Minister for Foreign Affairs was in a much better frame of mind that Halifax, and we soon came to an understanding. He even slightly complained of the British for their slowness and obstinacy.

Now the British Government was faced firmly with the choice: either—or. Chamberlain understood that at the present stage of development his new manœuvre (and he was thinking only of a manœuvre) was bound to include a triple pact. But, as further events showed, the Prime Minister remained unalterably loyal to his previous general policy.

Two days later, on May 24, he made a short statement in the House of Commons in which he assessed the immediate prospects with great optimism.

'I have every reason to hope that as a result of proposals which His Majesty's Government are now in a position to make on the main questions arising, it will be found possible to reach full agreement at an early date.'[1]

This hypocritical optimism was needed by Chamberlain at the time in order to calm British public opinion.

On May 25 Sir William Seeds, the British Ambassador in Moscow, handed the Soviet Government the new proposals of the British Government mentioned by Chamberlain in his Parliamentary statement.

1. Ibid., p. 668.

3

Two draft pacts

AND so, it seemed, the main difficulty in the negotiations had been overcome. The governments of Britain and France had at last recognized the necessity of concluding a triple pact of mutual assistance. True, on account of their opposition, manœuvres and hesitations ten weeks of valuable time had been lost to no purpose, but still it was not too late to arrest the hand of the aggressor raised to strike, if we acted quickly and resolutely.

That was exactly how the Soviet side was getting ready to act. We were thinking approximately on the following lines: 'The triple pact of mutual assistance has now been recognized in principle by both sides; the British and French know that we insist on guarantees for the Baltic States; we know that the British and French are insisting on guarantees for a number of countries in which they are particularly interested (Belgium, Greece, Turkey, etc.); in principle neither we nor they object to such guarantees—and consequently it will not be difficult to agree on this point; the desirability of the political pact and the supporting military convention entering into force simultaneously cannot arouse any doubts—and, consequently, on this point too it will be easy to arrive at a settlement. From all this it is clear that the prospects now opening are favourable, if, of course . . . both sides really want an agreement. We want it very much indeed . . . but what about the British and the French? . . .'

We hoped—or, more precisely, dared to hope—that even now, by the beginning of June, the British and French Governments had learned something, and had realized the necessity (even though it was for them a not quite pleasant necessity) of forming with the U.S.S.R. a united front against aggression. In any case we thought our political and historic duty, in spite of all the disappointments of the past, was once again to make an attempt to find a common language with the British and the French governments. And we did make it, convinced that with goodwill on both sides the triple pact of mutual assistance could be concluded in a very short time, and at all events in the course of June.

Unfortunately we were completely mistaken. Chamberlain and Daladier (I use the name of Daladier, here and later, as that not only of a person but also of the embodiment of the notorious '200 families') continued to hold firmly to their unswerving line of policy—of setting Germany on to the U.S.S.R. Even at this moment, when the dreadful spectre of a second world war could already be clearly seen on the horizon, they were thinking, most of all, not of how to conclude a triple pact as speedily as possible but of how to avoid signing it.

Did the British and French governments realize that a new 'leap' by Hitler was close at hand? Yes, they knew it, and I can bring convincing evidence of it. On June 12 I had an important conversation with Halifax, to which I shall return later. In the course of it I asked him how he thought the summer would pass? The British Foreign Secretary answered me in the following words (I quote his own record):

'It seemed to me that Herr Hitler would find it difficult to face the Nuremberg Conference without first having made an attempt to solve the Danzig problem, and that, if this were so, we must expect that July and August would be disturbed months.'[1]

As we see, the British Government understood perfectly well that a thunderstorm was looming ahead, and that on this occasion what was at stake was the fate of Poland, the integrity and independence of which Chamberlain and Daladier had just guaranteed. The British Government surely realized that without an agreement with the U.S.S.R. it could not save Poland. Yet in

---

1. *Documents on British Foreign Policy, 1919–1939*, Third Series, Vol. VI, p. 50. The 'Conference' Halifax had in mind was the big Fascist parade which the Hitlerites organized every year in September at Nuremberg.

spite of this, instead of concluding the triple pact as rapidly as possible, from the beginning of June it embarked on an obstinate sabotage of the very pact which it had officially just admitted to be necessary. The sad story of this sabotage will be told in the following pages. At this point I want to repeat that it is difficult in the annals of diplomacy to find another example of such double-dealing and hypocrisy as the behaviour of Chamberlain and Daladier in the tripartite negotiations of 1939. It is also difficult to find a more vivid example of political blindness dictated by class hatred. At the same time the attitude of the governments of Britain and France in the critical months of the negotiations testifies beyond all doubt that they were least of all concerned to save Poland, and that Poland, like Czechoslovakia the year before, was for them only a bargaining counter in their big game with Hitlerite Germany.

Recalling those days, I must include one more figure which played no small part in the Anglo-French sabotage of the tripartite negotiations—the figure of Joseph Kennedy, then Ambassador of the United States in London and father of the present President of the U.S.A.

Scion of a wealthy family, Joseph Kenedy made a rapid career as financier and business man, and by the time he was in his fifties had become very wealthy indeed. For his services to Franklin D. Roosevelt during his election campaign he had received the customary American recompense, and had arrived in Britain as Ambassador of the U.S.A. in 1938. Here he at once became one of the 'sensations' of the season—first of all as the father of nine children! That is not very frequent among members of the Diplomatic Corps. For several months the smiling face of the American Ambassador constantly adorned the pages of the newspapers and magazines—sometimes with his whole family, sometimes with his four sons, sometimes with his five daughters. Then began a campaign of honourary LL.D. degrees for Kennedy: six universities (Dublin, Edinburgh, Manchester, Birmingham, Bristol and Cambridge) conferred this honour upon the American Ambassador. On each occasion all kinds of praises were lavished upon him, and the photographers reproduced his likeness, now in his Doctor's gown, now without it, sometimes in his academic cap and sometimes bareheaded.

However, the American Ambassador devoted himself not only to society life and representative functions: he also took an active part in politics. And here he soon became the idol of the Cliveden set. Two main ideas dominated Kennedy's mind: faith in the might of Hitlerite Germany, disbelief in the vitality of Great Britain. As in addition the American Ambassador was far from benevolently inclined to the U.S.S.R., he naturally became the apostle of appeasement of the aggressors. He supported the policy of Chamberlain during the Czechoslovak crisis, and said after Munich that the British people should put up a statue to their Prime Minister for having saved Britain and Europe from war.

I recall how somewhat later, in June 1940, after France had capitulated and Britain was faced with the question of whether she should make peace with Germany or continue the war, Kennedy visited me at the Embassy and asked me what I thought about it. Kennedy himself was almost in a state of panic. He thought that Britain was powerless in face of Germany, that she had lost the war hopelessly and that the sooner she signed a peace with Hitler the better. The American Ambassador was very surprised when I began to disagree, and to prove to him that so far nothing was lost, that Britain still had great possibilities to resist successfully and to beat off the German threat, provided, of course, she retained her courage and readiness for struggle. I emphasized that, according to my own observations, the spirit of the great mass of the people was firm, and that even in the ruling class there were people who would not want to put up their hands in face of the impudent Fascist aggressors. Hence I drew the conclusion that it would be wrong to paint the prospect in exceptionally dark colours. When I had finished Kennedy with a gesture of surprise exclaimed:

'Well, you know, you are just an optimist. . . . I have never heard anything like this even from the British.'

Of course not! The only British with whom Kennedy mingled were British of the Cliveden brand, who believed neither in themselves nor in the future of their country.

However, at that moment there was in power in Britain a Government headed by Churchill. It had its defects, but nevertheless it better reflected the feeling of the masses: and Britain as a result did not capitulate to Hitlerite Germany. The American Ambassador and his friends wrung their hands in despair, but history has fully justified the decision of the British Government of that day.

It is easy to understand how a man like Kennedy could influence, and really did influence, the behaviour of the British in the tripartite negotiations of 1939. He was a faithful support for Chamberlain in all the complex gyrations of that lamentable affair.

On May 25 Seeds was sent new instructions. In keeping with them, the British Ambassador in Moscow and his French colleague Naggiar proposed their draft of a triple pact to the Soviet Government. Its essence was the following:

1. Britain, France and the U.S.S.R., 'acting in accordance with the principles of Article 16, paragraphs 1 and 2, of the Covenant of the League of Nations', would give one another all the support and assistance in their power in three cases: (a) should any of them be subjected to aggression on the part of a European Power: (b) if any of them were involved in military action as a result of a guarantee which it had given to any European State; and (c) if any of them were involved in military action as a result of assistance to any European State which, while not having a guarantee from the participants in the pact, had nevertheless requested such assistance in resisting aggression (Articles 1 and 2).

2. The three governments should discuss together the methods by which such mutual support and assistance would, in case of need, be made most effective (Article 3).

3. The pact was to remain in force for five years.[1]

1. *Documents on British Foreign Policy, 1919–1939*, Third Series, Vol. V, pp. 679–80.

Naturally, this draft could not at all satisfy the U.S.S.R. because of a number of defects. The principal among these were:

In the first place it linked the triple pact with the League of Nations. This meant in practice that, given the rules and manners dominating that organization at the time, the pact would never lead to quick and effective action. All would be confined to fine words and paper resolutions.

Secondly, it put the U.S.S.R. in an unequal position with its partners, obliging the U.S.S.R. to come to the aid of Britain and France if they were involved in war as a result of their guarantees to Poland, Rumania, Greece and some other States, but it did not bind Britain and France to come to the aid of the U.S.S.R. if the latter were involved in war as a result of an attack by Germany on the Baltic States, since Britain and France had not given them any guarantees. Yet the U.S.S.R. could always expect unpleasant surprises from that direction.

Finally, the clause about reinforcing the pact with a military convention was formulated in such general and indefinite terms that it was difficult to say when the military convention would be signed, and whether it would be signed at all. The impression was inevitably created that the British and French conceived of the pact as one more 'piece of paper' with which to speculate in their negotiations with Germany, but not as a real instrument for resisting aggression, armed with sharp teeth.

The content of the Anglo-French draft pact aroused melancholy reflections, and foreshadowed nothing good. Nevertheless the Soviet side decided to continue the negotiations in the hope of gradually straightening out the position. Therefore on June 2 the Soviet Government presented its partners in the negotiations with a counter-draft, the substance of which was the following:

1. France, Britain and the U.S.S.R. afford one another immediate and effective aid if any of them is involved in hostilities with a European Power in the event of:

(a) aggression by that Power against one of the signatories of the pact;

(b) aggression by that Power against Belgium, Greece,

Turkey, Rumania, Poland, Latvia, Estonia and Finland, whom Britain, France and the U.S.S.R. had undertaken to defend against aggression;

(c) assistance being granted by one of the signatories of the pact to any European Power (not among those guaranteed) which has requested such assistance in its struggle against violation of its neutrality.

2. In the event of joint military operations beginning as a result of the application of the pact, the three Powers which had signed it undertook not to conclude an armistice of peace except by common consent.

3. In the event of a threat of aggression arising on the part of a European Power, the three signatories would immediately consult and, should it become necessary, decide in common when and how the machinery of mutual assistance should be set in motion, irrespective of any procedure laid down by the League of Nations for the examination of this question.

4. The three signatories would as rapidly as possible conclude an agreement as to the methods, forms and dimensions of their mutual assistance. The pact would enter into force simultaneously with this agreement.

5. The pact was to be concluded for a five-year period.

It will be seen that the Soviet draft, while of a purely defensive character, eliminated the defects of the Anglo-French draft. It broke off its links with the League of Nations, it gave a precise list of States guaranteed by the three Great Powers, including the Baltic countries (i.e. it brought into being equality between the U.S.S.R. and its western partners) and it laid down firmly that the pact and the military convention would enter into force simultaneously. In addition, the Soviet draft pledged all participants in the pact, in the event of war, to conclude an armistice or sign peace only by common consent (though this latter point in the pact did not play any substantial part in the negotiations).

Had the governments of Britain and France been sincerely striving to set up a serious barrier in the way of Fascist aggression they should have welcomed the Soviet draft and accepted it

rapidly: for it fully guaranteed all the countries which they themselves had so far mentioned as particularly interesting them, and
it did in fact create an effective and rapidly operative machinery of
mutual assistance for resisting aggression.

Had they been. . . . But that was just the main condition which
was lacking! Chamberlain and Daladier were hypocritically
declaring that they wanted a pact, and even wanted it as soon as
possible, but in reality were cursing the day and hour when bitter
necessity had forced them to begin tripartite talks. That was just
why they had so pitilessly emasculated the very soul of the
pact in their draft of May 25. That was just why, when they met
with the Soviet counter-draft of June 2, they began a wearisome
and prolonged sabotage with the help of endless amendments,
reservations, additions and alterations. When they lost one
position in this process they clung to another, when they lost the
second they snatched at a third, and so on without end. The most
obvious things were suddenly subjected to question and doubt.
Under our pressure the British and French were forced constantly
to take step after step backwards: but they did it slowly, unwillingly, grinding their teeth and demanding on each occasion some
'compensation' from us for every such 'concession'.

When I remember that stifling, exhausting summer of 1939,
heavy with the electricity of thunderstorms, all those arguments,
conversations, meetings, discussions, disputes and compromises
in the atmosphere of which I had to pass that summer, I can in full
sincerity say that I have never had a more painful period in my
life. I felt that the world was rapidly sliding to disaster, that the
efforts of giants were necessary to avert a new world-wide
slaughter—and here before my eyes, on the banks of the Thames
and the Seine, pygmies were crawling about who did not want to
understand, and did not understand, what was going on in the
world, and who were living only for the day, sunk entirely in
petty moves and counter-moves of standard diplomatic routine.

4

To name or not to name

To be fair to the British and French, they speedily retreated on the question of the League of Nations, and even attempted to present matters as though differences had been caused by a pure misunderstanding: it wasn't that they had had in view that League procedure should be applied in connection with the triple pact, but, they alleged, it was only a question of putting on record, in the academic sense, that the pact was in keeping with the principles of the League of Nations. I had considerable doubts as to the sincerity of such an explanation, and a much greater part was probably played by the complete discrediting at this time of the League as an instrument for combatting aggression; nevertheless, it was a fact that in the first days of June this item in our differences had already disappeared. The Soviet side welcomed this step forward in the negotiations, but abstained for the time being from any guesses about the future.

On June 8 Halifax told me that, in order to accelerate the negotiations, he had decided to send to Moscow a prominent official of the Foreign Office, William Strang. This created a mixed impression. On the one hand, the dispatch of Strang, a man of intelligence and well acquainted with the Soviet Union through his past work there, seemed to bear witness to the desire of the British Government to reach agreement as rapidly as possible. On the other hand, it seemed somewhat strange that for such an important purpose instead of an important political personality an official (even if a capable one) of the diplomatic department should be sent. Halifax's information put me a little on my guard, but I did not wish to draw any premature conclusions. Therefore I simply put on record that on June 12 Strang left London by air and arrived in Moscow on June 14. Here he took an active part in the negotiations right up to the beginning of August.

In order to conclude the pact really quickly, as was our main aim, and at the same time to probe the genuine intentions of our British partners, the Soviet Government decided to invite Halifax to Moscow. However, not being certain of his attitute to such a step, it clothed its invitation in a more careful form. On the morning of June 12, the very day that Strang left for the U.S.S.R., I received an instruction to visit Halifax immediately and 'purely personally' and in friendly fashion to recommend him pressingly to come to Moscow as soon as possible in order to complete the negotiations and sign the pact. The same day I visited the Foreign Secretary and carried out my instructions. I said:

'Now that the sides have agreed on the most important question, and the pact of mutual assistance is to be concluded between the three States, it is most important that this necessary diplomatic act should be rounded off without any delay. The international situation is extremely tense, and events fraught with peril may occur in Danzig at any moment. . . . The forces of peace must hurry. . . . If the triple pact is signed in the next few days it may cool off Hitler considerably. . . . I think we are all interested in this. . . . Thinking over what could facilitate the speediest possible creation of a triple coalition against the aggressors, I have come to the conclusion that a great deal depends on you personally, Lord Halifax. If you were to agree immediately, this week or at latest next, to go to Moscow, to carry the negotiations through to the end there and sign the pact, peace in Europe would be preserved. Is not this task worthy of an important statesman, and ought not every possible effort be made to achieve it successfully? I can assure you quite definitely that the Soviet Government would welcome such a decision on your part, and you would meet with the warmest possible reception in Moscow.'

I watched Halifax attentively while I was speaking. His impassive face at first preserved its usual sceptical smile. As I went on, it adopted a more and more serious expression. Halifax was a sufficiently experienced diplomat to know that the Soviet Ambassador could not advise him so pressingly, even though it was 'purely in a personal capacity', to make the journey to Moscow if he had not had the sanction of his Government.

'If, Lord Halifax,' I concluded, 'you thought it possible to travel to Moscow now I would ask my Government to send you an official invitation.'

Halifax's expression became severe and enigmatic. He gazed attentively at the ceiling, then stroked the bridge of his nose and finally said with great significance:

'I will have this in mind.'

I understood, of course, that Halifax could not decide the question of going to Moscow without it being discussed in the Cabinet. I waited a few days; there was no reply to my invitation. A week went by—and Halifax continued to be silent. Now everything was clear: Halifax didn't want to go to Moscow, and the British Government was not dreaming of a rapid conclusion of the pact. Its agreement to sign a triple mutual assistance treaty, of which it had informed us on May 25, was not a sincere change in its views but a simple manœuvre imposed on it by circumstances. It would be quite impossible to put our trust in this agreement. In this way the Soviet Government had the reply to the question in which it had been interested: Halifax's passivity (for until the end of the negotiations he did not return to the question I had raised) was more eloquent than the most elaborate diplomatic statement.

Today, many years later, I can add a very important postscript to the conversation with Halifax on June 12, 1939, which I have just described. The *Documents on British Foreign Policy* published by the British Government contain a record of this conversation made by Halifax himself immediately afterwards. How does he represent there my invitation to him to come to Moscow? I quote the literal text of this record:

'7. In conclusion M. Maisky remarked that it would be a good thing if, when things were quieter, I were to go to Moscow myself, to which I replied that, whilst nothing, of course, would give me greater pleasure, I did not feel that it was possible for me at present to absent myself from London.'[1]

Leaving aside the fact that our fairly long talk about the journey was reduced here to a few very streamlined phrases, there are at least two definite untruths in Halifax's record, quoted here.

In the first place, I was insistently recommending Halifax to go to Moscow at once, in the middle of June, 1939, in order urgently to sign the pact and by that very means ensure that 'things were quieter' in Europe: whereas Halifax says exactly the opposite— that I was advising him to visit Moscow only after things 'became quieter', i.e. evidently after the signature of the pact. In essence the truth of my version is confirmed by Halifax himself, since in his record, stating what his reply was to my proposition, he says: 'I did not feel that it was possible for me at present to absent myself from London': in other words, what we were talking about was a visit by him 'at present', and not in some distant future.

Secondly, Halifax in his record asserts that he at once told me that it was impossible for him to go to Moscow at the time, when in reality the Foreign Secretary said nothing of the kind, replying only that he would keep my proposal in mind.

If the second untruth is not of particular importance, the first was a real and malicious falsification which completely distorted the truth. I don't know whether Halifax took his customary counsel with God before making the record of our conversation, but there is no doubt on this point that the Noble Lord on this occasion behaved in quite unworthy fashion.

The question obviously arises, why did he need to do this? My explanation is that as the records of conversations with Ambassadors were usually circulated to all members of the Cabinet, Halifax wished to conceal my invitation even from his Ministerial colleagues, lest it might cause internal complications among the members of the Government. For at that time the whole foreign policy of Great Britain was in effect concentrated in the hands of

1. *Documents on British Foreign Policy, 1919–1939*, Third Series, Vol. VI, p. 51.

three men—Chamberlain, Horace Wilson and Halifax, and the
role of Wilson was moreover much more important than that of
Halifax.

The accuracy of my supposition is confirmed by one other
striking fact. About the same time, learning of Halifax's unwillingness to go to Moscow, Eden on his own initiative offered his
services to the British Government.

'I have reason to believe,' he stated, 'that the Russians are not
unfriendly disposed towards me. . . . If for some reason it is
inconvenient for Lord Halifax to go to Moscow at present, send
me and charge me with the completion of the negotiations.'

However, the Chamberlain Government rejected Eden's
proposal.[1]

And so we now knew that the British Government had had no
change of heart, and that it remained true as before to the political
line of the Clivedenites. None the less the Soviet Government
decided to continue the negotiations despite all, and to carry
through to the bitter end its attempt to assure peace by the
creation of a triple coalition. This was dictated by the interests of
the Soviet people and of all mankind. It was dictated by our
responsibility to history.

I have not the space here to describe in all its details—nor is it
really necessary—that scurrying as of many mice around the
triple pact with the help of which the British and French governments in the summer of 1939 sabotaged a successful outcome of
the negotiations. I will only say that I felt all the time as though
we, the Soviet side, were bursting through a thick and prickly
mass of bushes, in which at every step we were also encountering
ruts and pitfalls. Our clothes were being torn to rags, our faces,
hands and legs were being covered with deep scratches and even
bleeding wounds, but all the same we were stubbornly pressing

    1. In the summer of 1939 only a few vague rumours reached me about
this attempt by Eden to put matters right. Much later, when the war was in
progress, Eden himself told me about the failure of his attempt. Mention is
made of this by Neville Chamberlain's biographer, Keith Feiling (op cit.,
p. 409), and by Winston Churchill (op. cit., Vol. I, 1948 edition, p. 303).

forward to the aim we had set ourselves. . . . Alas, we never reached it—and what I have to relate will show why. At present I will dwell only on the main stages of those negotiations.

The whole of June passed in dispute (only to think of it!) about whether the countries which the three Great Powers were to guarantee should or should not be named in the text of the pact. As I pointed out earlier, the Anglo-French draft of May 25 contained a clause binding Britain, France and the U.S.S.R. to come to one another's assistance in the event of their being involved in war as guarantors of some European State. This was too general and indeterminate a formula, which in practice permitted of various interpretations. Had relations between the Soviet Government on the one hand and the French and British governments on the other been founded on friendship and mutual confidence we might possibly have reconciled ourselves to this formula. But in fact the relations between these governments were full of mutual distrust and suspicion, for which the Soviet Government, as we know, had more than adequate grounds. Therefore the U.S.S.R., in its counter-draft of June 2, mentioned precisely the eight countries which the three Great Powers undertook to guarantee. They were (I venture to repeat them) Belgium, Greece, Turkey, Rumania, Poland, Latvia, Estonia and Finland. Here the interests both of the U.S.S.R. and of Britain and France were being taken into account. It might have seemed that Chamberlain and Daladier should have been satisfied. But no, they were discontented. With what?

First, that the three Baltic States had been introduced among the countries guaranteed. Why was that necessary? It was an extra burden! The British and French governments tried in various ways to convince us that such a guarantee was unnecessary, and incidentally laid special stress on the assertion that the territory of the Baltic States was too narrow to permit of the creation of an effective military front. Consequently it could not be made use of by the Germans against the U.S.S.R. without simultaneously the front being extended to the territory of Poland. And if Poland were involved in the war the guarantee

K

given her by Britain and France would enter into force. Naturally, the Soviet Government could not accept such arguments, and, in that same conversation with Halifax on June 12 which I mentioned earlier, I said plainly that without a guarantee for the three Baltic States there would be no pact.

When after this the British and French had to withdraw their objections to guarantees for the Baltic countries they suddenly said that they considered undesirable any mention by name in the text of the pact of the States which were being guaranteed. Why? All kinds of arguments were brought forward. An open guarantee would allegedly offend the national pride of the guaranteed country. An open guarantee would allegedly frighten the guaranteed States, for it would create the impression that they were being included in the anti-Hitler front. An open guarantee without the direct consent of the guaranteed States would allegedly be an infringement of the principles of international law.

When the Soviet side in reply suggested that Britain and France should exercise their influence in the States to be guaranteed, and should induce their governments at least not to object to the guarantees, Chamberlain and Daladier would immediately strike a solemn attitude and proclaim that every State was sovereign, and therefore it would be sinful to suggest that it should participate in the anti-Hitler front. More than that, our partners in the negotiations—particularly the British—incited (officially or unofficially) the reactionary governments of the Baltic States to make open declarations that they did not want to receive any guarantees of any kind from the three Great Powers. In fact, the Foreign Ministers of Finland, Estonia and Latvia did issue declarations in this sense, and with particular belligerency in the case of Estonia.

Then the Soviet Government drew the logical conclusion from the situation which had been created. On June 16 the People's Commissar for Foreign Affairs invited the British and French Ambassadors to renounce any mention at all of guarantees for other European States, and simply sign a triple pact of mutual assistance between Britain, France and the U.S.S.R. in the event of a direct attack by Germany on one of the three Powers.

This aroused great concern in London and Paris. They began to argue: 'If the Soviet proposal is accepted what will become of the guarantees to Poland and Rumania which were given by Britain and France in March and April, 1939? They will be left in the air and become mere scraps of paper, capable however of dealing a very sensible blow to the prestige of the Powers which gave them.' Therefore the British and French governments hastened to reject the conclusion of a simple pact of mutual assistance, and once again returned to a pact with guarantees for other countries. At a number of sessions in Moscow they tried in various ways to avoid the necessity of naming the guaranteed countries in the pact, and when they became convinced that this was impossible, on June 21, they put forward the proposal (in practice it was made by the French Ambassador Naggiar) that the list of guaranteed countries should be transferred from Article I of the main text of the pact to a secret protocol attached to the pact.[1] It was not quite comprehensible why this seemed more suitable to the British and French, because in our day the content of every secret document very soon becomes common knowledge: but since our partners were insisting on such a protocol, the Soviet Government did not think it necessary to object.

In this connection I think it useful to make a remark about the relations between the British and French in the course of the tripartite negotiations. I have already mentioned the comment of Y. Z. Suritz, our Ambassador in Paris, that, for all its reactionary character, the Daladier Government had nevertheless a more favourable attitude to the pact than the Chamberlain Government, This was to be explained, of course, not by any particular nobility of character or far-sightedness of the French Munichites, but by the fact that Germany was a much more direct menace to France than to Britain. However that might be, in spite of all the identity

1. *Documents on British Foreign Policy, 1919–1939,* Third Series, Vol. VI, pp. 140–2.

of the line pursued by London and Paris in the negotiations there were differences in shades of opinion between them, which made their appearance from time to time. It was this in particular that showed itself on the question of enumerating the guaranteed countries, when Naggiar made his proposal for transferring their names to a secret protocol. It will be seen later that this occurred more than once.

However, the affair of naming the guaranteed countries was by no means at an end. When the question of a secret protocol had been agreed the British and French suddenly stated that they wanted the guarantee to be extended to three more countries in which they were interested—Holland, Luxembourg and Switzerland. In this way it turned out that the three Great Powers must now guarantee not eight countries, as had been presumed in all the negotiations hitherto, but eleven countries, among whom two, Holland and Switzerland, did not even maintain diplomatic relations with the U.S.S.R.

This naturally was bound to increase the burden devolving on the guarantors, and particularly the U.S.S.R., for it was the U.S.S.R. which in the event of war would have to bear the main burden of the guarantee for six of the States—Poland, Rumania, Turkey and the three Baltic States. The Soviet side at one of the sessions pointed out that already the obligations in respect of the eight States first provided for, translated into military terms, would require if they had to be carried out that the U.S.S.R. should put 100 divisions into the field, and if the number of guaranteed countries were extended still more would be needed. In view of this the Soviet Government expressed its readiness to extend the protection of the Big Three to the three additional States only if it received a certain 'compensation' in the shape, for example, of pacts of mutual assistance with Poland and Turkey, instead of the unilateral guarantees to these States by the Soviet Union, as previously provided. Britain and France at once hid themselves again behind the sovereignty of Poland and Turkey, and moreover, with such an attitude on their part, it was clear that pacts of mutual assistance with the two countries mentioned would be extremely problematical. It was decided, therefore, in the end that Holland, Luxembourg and Switzerland would, after all, not be included in the list of guaranteed countries, but that the secret protocol mentioned earlier would say that in the event of a threat to the independence of these three States arising, the members of the Big Three would consult as to the measures which should be taken.

The British and French not only endlessly dragged out the negotiations, they also demanded that we should 'compensate' them for every 'concession' they made. On this subject I had a sharp encounter with Halifax on June 23. Inviting me to the Foreign Office, Halifax began bitterly complaining of Soviet 'stubbornness' and 'obstinacy', and then, with the severe and enigmatic expression I had seen before, asked me bluntly whether the Soviet Government really wanted a triple pact.

'Why do you ask such a question?' I said. 'You know perfectly that the Soviet Government is a convinced partisan of a triple pact.'

'I don't see this,' said Halifax. 'In all negotiations both sides make concessions, and in the end agree on a compromise. We, the British side, have made many concessions to you in the course of these negotiations, but you have not moved one iota from your original position. . . . Obviously the Soviet Government is not interested in the pact.'

'Excuse me, Lord Halifax,' I retorted. 'There must be different conceptions on the Soviet and British sides as to what are diplomatic negotiations. The British side evidently conceives of them as something like a bazaar in which two merchants are haggling: first the merchants incredibly inflate their prices, then gradually begin to lower them, and finally they arrive at an agreement—and in the process each merchant demands, for every concession he has made, a similar concession from his partner. . . . Well, we, the Soviet side, have a somewhat different view of diplomatic negotiations. We don't try at first to make demands beyond all measure in order to have something afterwards to "yield". We say straight away what, in our opinion, is needed to reach the objective aimed at. We have acted in this way in these negotiations too. What was set out in the Soviet draft on June 2 was that "iron minimum" which can ensure peace in Europe. You, on the other hand, began with what could not in any way assure this peace, and therefore naturally had gradually to move in our direction, because you too should be interested in preserving European peace.

'We cannot depart from our "iron minimum" without betraying the cause of peace,' I continued, 'while you need still to come a little closer to us, so that with our joint strength we should be in a position to set the limit to aggression. Therefore you had better put away your catalogue of those concessions you have made, and don't ask us for any compensations for them. We shall not make them. We are realists. Please understand that we are interested not in juridical formulae, not an equilibrium of concessions on one side and the other; we are interested in the essence of the case, that is, real prevention of aggression and assurance of peace in Europe. To achieve this objective there is only one way—the way along which the Soviet side is going. Let's go along it together.'

Halifax heard me out attentively, but would not agree. He began now to prove to me that in all negotiations the 'human element' is very important, and this 'element' implies an obligation of mutual concessions. Without such mutual concessions there cannot come into being an 'atmosphere' which promotes the successful course and outcome of negotiations. We were making a mistake if we were ignoring the question of 'atmosphere'.

'After hearing your views,' I summed up, 'I am ready perhaps to admit that the Soviet Government has really made one mistake: it did not take into account the "bazaar methods" of British diplomacy, and therefore revealed too early and too frankly its "iron minimum". But really we have no grounds to apologize for this mistake.'

The longer negotiations went on, the more clear it became that the British and French were simply applying tactics of sabotage. The European situation was becoming more heated day by day.

The thunder-cloud was obviously gathering over Danzig. On June 18 Goebbels arrived there, and made a frenzied speech in which he stated openly that the time was coming when Danzig would become part of Hitlerite Germany. During the following days thousands of German 'tourists' flooded into the city. Vast quantities of arms of all kinds, even heavy artillery, were delivered there by contraband. Foerster, the Nazi leader in Danzig, made an appeal to the population to spare no effort to turn it once again into a German city. Under the influence of all these events the tension in German-Polish relations grew, and so did excitement in London and Paris. Speaking in Parliament on June 27, Daladier said that 'never yet had Europe been in such a state of confusion and alarm as at present', and five days later, on July 2, the French Prime Minister recognized that 'the general situation in Europe is extremely serious'. In a speech on June 28, in London, Churchill said that he was very concerned with the situation in which they were at present. It was very similar to that of the previous year—with this difference, however, that now there was no possibility of retreat. Britain had not been tied by any treaty to Czechoslovakia. But now she had given an absolute guarantee to Poland. Everything pointed to the fact that the Nazis had made the necessary preparations in order to force Poland to yield. If she did not yield she would be attacked by great forces from the west and the south.

Even Halifax himself, in a speech on June 29, drew the prospects opening before Europe in very gloomy colours.

Yet in spite of all this the British and French governments continued to drag on their wearisome, artificially thought-up delays in the negotiations for a triple pact. One of their favourite methods in this respect was to hold up their replies to our proposals or amendments. It was just at this time that I made a small statistical calculation of how long had been taken during the negotiations for the Soviet and Anglo-French sides respectively to prepare their replies. The resulting figures were very interesting. It turned out that out of the seventy-five days which the negotiations had by that time occupied, the U.S.S.R. had taken

only sixteen days, while Britain and France had taken fifty-nine.
Not surprisingly, these figures were used in the Soviet press. In
an article which appeared in *Pravda* on June 29, 1939, it was
stated:

'The Anglo-Franco-Soviet negotiations for the conclusion of
an effective pact of mutual assistance against aggression have
entered a blind alley. . . .

'The fact of the intolerable delays and endless pretexts for
dragging out the negotiations gives ground for doubt of the
sincerity of the true intentions of Britain and France. It obliges us
to consider what precisely is at the bottom of such a policy—
serious aspirations to ensure a peace front, or the desire to make
use of the fact of the negotiations, and of the dragging out of the
negotiations themselves, for some other purposes which have
nothing in common with the cause of the creation of a front of
peace-loving Powers.

'Such a question arises all the more because in the course of the
negotiations the British and French governments are piling up
artificial difficulties, creating the appearance of serious differences
between Britain and France on the one hand and the U.S.S.R. on
the other, over questions which, given good will and sincere
intentions on the part of Britain and France, could be resolved
without delay and without difficulty.'

Pointing further to one such 'artificial difficulty' (the question
of guarantees for the Baltic States) and underlining that in other
cases, where Britain felt herself really interested (the question of
guarantees for Holland and others) she reckoned very little with
the wishes of the countries which she was undertaking to
guarantee, *Pravda* continued:

'The British and French do not want an agreement with the
U.S.S.R. based on the principle of equality and reciprocity,
though they swear every day that they too are for "equality"; they
want an agreement in which the U.S.S.R. would act as their hired
labourer, bearing on its own shoulders all the burden of the
obligations undertaken.'

Declaring that there could be no question of such an agreement,

Pravda concluded its article with the following very significant words:

'It would seem that the British and French want, not a real agreement acceptable to the U.S.S.R., but only *talk* about an agreement—in order, by speculating on the imaginary rigidity of the U.S.S.R. in face of the public opinion of their countries, to facilitate a deal with the aggressors.'

This was straight talking.

5

Pact and military convention

HOWEVER that might be, by the beginning of July the question of enumerating the States guaranteed by the three Great Powers had been settled. The time had come to solve the other problems before signature was possible. Most important among them was the question of a link between the pact and the supporting military convention. It cannot be said that this question had not been raised earlier: not by any means. It had already been referred to more than once in the course of June, during the conversations between the Soviet, British and French representatives in Moscow, and also between myself and Halifax in London. Nevertheless, in June the main efforts of each side were concentrated on the question of whether the States guaranteed by the Big Three should or should not be named.

Now in July the question of the military convention came up into the foreground. There were special grounds for this. The atmosphere in Europe was now terribly tense, war might break out at any time, and it was necessary to establish as rapidly and as exactly as possible what help the three Great Powers would give one another if any of them were involved in war with Germany. During the negotiations with the Anglo-French representatives in Moscow it was more than once underlined that a pact without a military convention was 'an empty piece of paper', and that in the situation which had arisen a military convention was more important than the pact. However, on this question too our partners with obstinate blindness pursued the same tactics of sabotage, even though the ground was becoming hot under their very feet.

The attitude of the two sides on the question of the pact and the military convention was essentially the following.

The Soviet Government considered that the pact and the military convention should represent an integral whole, two parts of one and the same agreement, entering into force simultaneously. In other words, without a military convention there could not be any political pact. This point of view had been clearly expressed in our very first proposals of April 17, and we had consistently maintained it in all our conversations with the British and the French, whether in Moscow, London or Paris. I have already explained why we were obliged strictly to adhere to this point of view.

The British and French governments, on the contrary, considered that the pact and the military convention were two different documents, and that it was undesirable to bind them together too closely. Why? When in conversation with Halifax on June 8 I first touched on this question the British Foreign Secretary said:

'To require the simultaneous entry into force of the pact and the military convention would mean considerably delaying the signature of an agreement. . . . A military convention is not worked out so speedily. . . . Any delay would be dangerous for the cause of peace. . . . We must hurry!'

And Halifax urged that the pact should first be concluded and then the military convention should be considered. I did not agree with this, but as at that moment it was most important of all for us to come to terms about the enumeration of the States guaranteed by the pact, the problem of its relation with the military convention was postponed until a more appropriate moment. Later on both the British and the French invariably maintained the point of view set out by Halifax in this conversation, constantly repeating: 'A military convention will only delay the conclusion of the pact, and we must hurry, hurry on. . . . The international situation is assuming such a threatening character!'

It is difficult to imagine a more vivid example of double-faced, hypocritical behaviour. What was the true reason for this behaviour of the British and French governments?

It consisted in the same unchanged devotion to the general line of the Clivedenites and the consequent dislike of a triple pact of mutual assistance. It was just at this time, at the beginning of July, that I was told of an exchange between Chamberlain and his close friend Sir Kingsley Wood, Air Minister:

'How are the negotiations for a pact going on?' asked Kingsley Wood.

Chamberlain replied irritably: 'I still have not lost hope that we shall not have to sign this deplorable pact.'

If such was the state of mind of the head of the Government one can scarcely be surprised at the unwillingness of Halifax and Daladier to consider the pact and the military convention as an inseparable whole.

But as, at the beginning of July, the Soviet Government categorically put this question before them, the British and French governments had willy-nilly to take it up.

On July 12 Halifax asked me to come and see him, and once again began arguing about the undesirability of the simultaneous entry into force of the pact and the military convention. However, I interrupted him at once, and said that it was useless to argue about this, because the Soviet Government would not in any circumstances sign a pact without a convention. Halifax asked what was the reason for our obstinacy on this question. In reply I briefly told him of our unsuccessful experience with the Franco-Soviet Pact of Mutual Assistance. The Soviet Government had firmly decided that nothing like this should happen again, all the more because times now were much more dangerous than in 1935.

Halifax was silent for a few moments, plunged in meditation, and then, with a side-long glance at me, said with an air of great significance:

'That means that you don't trust us?'

I shrugged my shoulders and replied:

'Three great States are coming to an agreement about very important things, and it should all be precise and clear. Otherwise there may arise the most undesirable misunderstandings and disputes.'

In Moscow the Soviet Government persistently defended the conception of a single agreement in two parts, and in order to gain time suggested that negotiations for a military convention should begin immediately, without waiting for the final conclusion of a pact. The political negotiations could continue parallel with this. This proposal did not please Halifax at all; but the Soviet side was firmly maintaining the attitude that there would either be a simultaneous pact and convention or no pact at all. As a result, Halifax had already in the middle of July given Seeds the directive to agree to the interdependence of pact and convention, and also to the early commencement of talks about the latter: but gave the Ambassador the right himself to decide when to inform the Soviet side of this. Seeds, on his part, dragged matters on for another week, and only at the meeting of July 24 informed the Soviet People's Commissar that the British Government did not object to the immediate opening of negotiations for a military convention. The Soviet Government proposed that they should take place in Moscow.

In this way, thanks to the sabotage of our partners, three more weeks were needed to settle the question of the link between the pact and the military convention.

But this was not yet all. Now, when the two questions— enumerating the guaranteed States and integrating the pact and the military convention—had been settled, another difficulty had to be overcome. It was necessary to give a more precise definition of what was meant by aggression. Three Great Powers were undertaking to come to the help of eight other countries if they became victims of aggression: but how was the term 'aggression' to be understood?

And so an endless new palaver began once again. The Soviet Government took up a very conciliatory position on this question. It took full account of the objections of our partners and frequently made concessions to them, altering and re-fashioning its proposals; but all in vain. The suspicious eye of Halifax invariably discovered in any formulation some word or comma which aroused in him a negative reaction. The arguments about definition of aggression went on all through July and continued in August, without bringing us to any agreement. They had not been finished when the tripartite negotiations collapsed altogether.

Here I must mention again the differences which arose between the British and the French in the course of the talks. A telegram from Seeds on July 22 contains the following paragraph:

'French Ambassador's personal view is that M. Molotov's definition of indirect aggression (my telegram No. 157) could be accepted, and he would intimate to us privately that this is in fact the view of the French Government, though they have agreed reluctantly to support His Majesty's Government in their objection to it.'[1]

Simultaneously, on the same July 22, Halifax was cabling to Seeds:

'There have been press reports in Paris and London to the effect that French Government are prepared to meet M. Molotov at all points and have been urging His Majesty's Government in vain to fall into line. If subject is raised you may inform your French colleague that we have every reason to believe that leakage is from French sources.'[2]

The question of the source of the leakage was of secondary importance. Much more important was the fact that, the longer the negotiations were dragged out through Chamberlain's machinations, the more obvious became the differences between London and Paris.

Observing the conduct of the British side day by day, during the discussions on the definition of aggression, we involuntarily returned again and again to the question, could a Government behave in this way if it really wanted to conclude a triple pact as soon as possible? And every time we were obliged to reply: 'No, it could not: evidently the British Government, as before, does not wish to conclude a pact.'

In July there was an important event which still further

1. *Documents on British Foreign Policy, 1919–1939*, Third Series, Vol. VI, p. 450.
2. Ibid., pp. 448–9.

deepened our doubts as to the sincerity of our British partner. About the 20th of that month Mr. Hudson, Secretary of the Department of Overseas Trade, had a meeting with Goering's adviser on economic questions, Helmuth Wohlthat. Officially Wohlthat had come to London to take part in an international conference of the Whaling Commission; but in fact his task was to make soundings as to the possibility of a broad settlement of relations between Britain and Germany. At that time we did not know all the details of Wohlthat's conversations with British official personalities. We did not know, in particular (this transpired only after the war), of the talks which Wohlthat had with Sir Horace Wilson. In the record made by von Dirksen, then the German Ambassador in London, on July 21, 1939, we find the following data as to the conversations between Wohlthat and Hudson and Horace Wilson:

Hudson had asked Wohlthat, through the Norwegian member of the Whaling Commission, to come and see him. During the talks Hudson developed far-reaching plans for Anglo-German co-operation in opening up new world markets and exploiting existing ones. In particular, he said that Britain and Germany could find wide opportunities for their activity in China, Russia and the British Empire. Hudson thought it was essential to delimit the spheres of British and German interests.

Then, on the initiative of Sir Horace Wilson, Wohlthat visited him too. The two conversations between Wohlthat and Chamberlain's principal adviser on foreign policy were of a more all-round character. Wilson stated that his purpose was 'a broad Anglo-German agreement on all important questions', and in particular (a) the conclusion of an Anglo-German pact of non-aggression, (b) the conclusion of a pact of non-intervention and delimitation of spheres of influence, (c) limitation of land, naval and air armaments, (d) the granting to Germany of the possibility of joining in exploitation of the colonies and (e) mutual financial assistance and problems of international trade. When Wohlthat asked whether the German Government could put down other questions for discussion as well, Wilson answered 'that the

Fuehrer had only to take a sheet of paper and jot down his points; the British Government would be prepared to discuss them.' Wilson asked that Hitler should authorize some person to negotiate on all the questions bearing on Anglo-German co-operation.

Dirksen also recorded: 'Sir Horace Wilson definitely told Herr Wohlthat that the conclusion of a non-aggression pact [with Germany I.M.] would enable Britain to rid herself of her commitments vis-à-vis Poland.'[1]

Wilson suggested that Wohlthat should have an immediate conversation with Chamberlain in order to convince himself that the latter agreed with the programme which had been developed to Wohlthat. But the latter avoided a meeting with the British Prime Minister.

Such were the conversations which Chamberlain carried on with Germany in the summer of 1939, behind the back of the U.S.S.R. If nothing came of them in the long run this was the result of factors over which the British Prime Minister had no control. All this, and western historians and politicians have the audacity to cast a stone at the Soviet Government, accusing it of conspiracy and almost alliance with Germany behind the backs of Britain and France! Even if the Soviet Government had acted in this way it would have only been paying back the western democracies in their own coin. But in reality, as will be shown later, it did not do anything of the kind. I repeat that in the summer of 1939 we did not yet know the details of the secret conversations between the governments of Britain and Hitlerite Germany. However, what did percolate into the press and political circles in July, 1939, was quite sufficient to create serious concern. As the newspapers wrote then, and as Chamberlain admitted in his Parliamentary statement of July 24, Hudson and Wohlthat had talked of the expansion of Anglo-German commercial and financial relations, and of the granting by Britain to Germany, on definite terms, of a vast loan of the order of £500–1,000 millions.

1. *Documents and Materials Relating to the Eve of the Second World War* (English edition, Moscow, 1948), Vol. II, pp. 67–72.

A commercial deal on this scale was of first-class political signifi-cance. If a member of the British Government thought it possible to discuss such a scheme with an important official of the Hitlerite State did it not mean . . . ? But we did not draw too far-reaching conclusions. Naturally, our distrust of the true intentions of the British Government, which had grown up as a result of all our previous experience—and particularly of the experience of the tripartite negotiations—was only increased.

6

Preparing for the military negotiations

ON JULY 25 Halifax invited me to come and see him, and told
me of the agreement reached in Moscow to begin military conversations immediately. I knew this already from a telegram of the
People's Commissariat for Foreign Affairs which I had received
earlier, but nevertheless expressed great satisfaction at the
Foreign Secretary's communication. I was still worried by some
doubts, however, and tried at once to find out to what extent they
were justified.

'Tell me, Lord Halifax,' I asked, 'when in your opinion can
these negotiations begin?'

Halifax pondered, looked at the ceiling as though casting up
something in his mind, and then replied:

'We shall need at least a week or ten days to do all the necessary
preliminary work.'

This meant that in practice the negotiations could hardly begin
for a fortnight. So Halifax did not intend to hurry.

'And have the members of your mission for the military
negotiations already been selected?' I asked again.

'No, not yet. . . . We shall do this in the next few days,' said
Halifax. Then he added: 'We think the most convenient place for
the military talks would be Paris, but as the Soviet Government
has expressed the wish that they should be conducted in Moscow
we are ready to meet there.'

I left Halifax with a feeling of great alarm: the old game was
going on, while the international situation was becoming worse
and worse. The militarization of Danzig was going on at an
increasing tempo, and the strain on Polish-German relations was

becoming almost intolerable. On July 21 the German Ministry for Foreign Affairs declared that Danzig must be returned to Germany 'without any conditions'. To this the leader of the Polish Army, Marshal Rydz-Smigly, replied that if Germany attempted to settle the fate of Danzig unilaterally Poland would take up arms. About the same time the British General Ironside visited Warsaw and had talks there with the Polish General Staff. Serious events were also taking place in the Far East. The Sino-Japanese war had been going on already for two years, and no end to it could be seen. At Khalkhin-Gol battles were going on between the Japanese aggressors and the Soviet-Mongol forces. The Japanese imperialists were carrying on a furious campaign against Britain in China, bombing her ships on the Yangtse, organizing hostile demonstrations in Chinese cities and threatening British citizens resident there with death. All this was arousing tremendous alarm in Britain, and broad masses of the people, in particular the workers, were attacking the Government more and more violently for its sabotage of the tripartite negotiations. From end to end of the whole country there was a loud demand for an immediate pact with the Soviet Union.

Chamberlain once again had to wriggle out of the situation. On July 31 there was a stormy foreign policy debate in the House of Commons. Sir Archibald Sinclair, leader of the Liberals, sharply criticized Chamberlain's policy, and demanded that 'a person of the highest political rank' should be sent to Moscow to complete the negotiations for the pact. Dalton, on behalf of the Labour Party, suggested that Halifax himself should go to Moscow, or that a member of the Soviet Government be invited to London. Eden insisted on the urgent dispatch of a political mission headed by someone of such standing that he could deal direct with the Soviet Government. Many other members spoke in the same spirit.

Beating off these attacks on the sabotage of negotiations, Chamberlain was minded to call in precedents from the past He said that negotiations for the Anglo-Japanese Alliance in 1903 took six months, negotiations for the Anglo-French Entente of

1904 went on for nine months, negotiations for the Anglo-Russian Entente of 1907 took fifteen months. .... The conclusion to be drawn was obvious: 'The present negotiations with the U.S.S.R. have been going on only four and a half months, what do you expect?'[1] It is difficult to imagine a more striking example of political thick-headedness than these arguments of the British Prime Minister in conditions of the historic storm which had almost begun.

In spite of the widespread indignation of British public opinion, Chamberlain continued to stand by his original line of policy. He still had not lost hope of bringing Germany and the U.S.S.R. into conflict. All the actions of the British Government, even at that late hour, spoke clearly of this.

After my conversation with Halifax on July 25 I made an attempt to influence the composition of the military delegation which Britain was intending to send to the U.S.S.R. I argued: 'Even if Halifax did not go to Moscow in June, let today, at any rate, the chief representative of Britain be some really prominent and active military figure. This would be valuable for the negotiations themselves; it might somewhat cool the aggressive ardour of Hitler; it would be evidence of a serious attitude to the triple pact on the part of Britain if even now, on the very threshold of war, there took place some change for the better in the attitude of its ruling group.'

I turned to Arthur Greenwood, Deputy Leader of the Labour Party in Parliament, with whom I had good relations, and asked him unofficially to let the British Government know that the Soviet side hoped to see a very prominent military man at the head of the British delegation—best of all General Gort, who was then Chief of the British General Staff. I know for certain that Greenwood carried out my request. In reply he received a letter from Chamberlain (I have read it myself) in which the Prime Minister stated that the Government unfortunately could not send Lord Gort to Moscow, as he was too much required at the moment in London: but that the delegation would be headed instead by

1. *Parliamentary Debates. House of Commons*, Vol. 350, Col. 2023.

someone who would command the necessary 'respect' of the Soviet Government.

And what was the result? On July 31 Chamberlain announced in Parliament that the Cabinet had placed leadership of the British military delegation in the hands of Sir Reginald Plunkett Ernle-Erle-Drax. I must admit that I had never heard his name before during all my seven years of previous work as Soviet Ambassador in London. That was not surprising. It turned out that Sir Reginald Plunkett Drax had no operative relation to the British armed forces at that time whatever, but in return was close to the Court and Chamberlainite in his inclinations. Even had one wished, it would have been difficult to find a candidate more unsuited to conduct negotiations with the U.S.S.R. than this elderly British Admiral. The other members of the delegation, Air Marshal Sir Charles Burnett and Major-General Heywood, did not rise above the average level of the leading personnel in the British land forces.

When I learned of the composition of the British delegation I could only draw the conclusion that everything remained as it was, and the sabotage of a triple pact would continue.

The French Government took the line indicated for it by its London colleagues: General d'Armée Doumenc was appointed head of the delegation, and General Valin, of the Air Force, and Capitaine de Corvette Willaume were members. Here too there was not one of them who could speak with authority on behalf of all the armed forces of his country. At the beginning of August the French delegation arrived in London, whence they were to travel together to Moscow. I decided to give a luncheon for them: however disappointed I was in the composition of the delegations, diplomatic politeness required such a gesture on my part. Moreover, I wanted to have a personal talk with the members of the delegations. The luncheon was held in the former conservatory of the Embassy. In addition to the British and French delegations there were also present our military personnel (the military, air and naval attachés) and responsible officials of our Trade Delegation. To my right, as senior among the guests, sat

Admiral Drax, a tall, lean, grey-headed Englishman, tranquil in his movements and unhasty in speech. When luncheon was over and coffee had been served the following conversation took place between us:

MAISKY: Tell me, Admiral, when are you leaving for Moscow?

DRAX: It has not yet been finally decided, but in the next few days.

MAISKY: You are flying, of course? . . . There is not much time, the situation in Europe is very tense!

DRAX: Oh no, there are about forty of us in the two delegations, if you reckon the technical staff, and we have a lot of baggage. . . . It wouldn't be convenient to go by plane.

MAISKY: Well, if it isn't suitable by plane, I hope you are going to the Soviet Union on one of your fast cruisers. It would be very much in style and very impressive: military delegations on a warship. . . . And it wouldn't take much time from London to Leningrad.

DRAX: (beginning to look sour): No, a cruiser wouldn't be suitable either. If we were to go by cruiser it would mean depriving a couple of dozen of its officers of their cabins. . . . Why should we put people to such inconvenience? . . . No, we won't be going by cruiser.

MAISKY: But in that event perhaps you will take one of your fast-going commercial vessels? I must repeat that this is a very urgent moment, you ought to be in Moscow as quickly as possible!'

DRAX (obviously unwilling to continue this conversation any further): Really, I can't tell you anything definitely. The Board of Trade is organizing the transport. Everything is in its hands. I don't know what is going to happen.

And what happened was the following. On August 5 the military delegation sailed from London on a cargo and passenger steamer, *City of Exeter*, making thirteen knots, and arrived at last in Leningrad only on August 10. Five whole days had passed on the journey, at a time when hours and even minutes counted on the scales of history! At that time I imagined that the phenomenal delay in arranging and dispatching the delegations to the U.S.S.R. was one of the expressions of that spirit of sabotage with which we were only too well acquainted. Undoubtedly, on the whole, I was right. But today, from the diplomatic documents published by the British Government, it can be seen that there was also a special purpose in the leisurely manner in which Drax and his colleagues were making their way to Moscow. I have already said that when agreement was reached between the two sides for the immediate beginning of military talks the political pact had not yet been completely elaborated: the question of defining the conception of 'aggression' had yet to be settled. It was proposed that the political and military negotiations would go on simultaneously. And so, in the written instructions given by the Foreign Office as a guidance to the delegation during the Moscow negotiations, clause 8 read:

'Until such time as the political agreement is concluded the Delegation should go very slowly with the conversations, watching the progress of the political negotiations and keeping in very close touch with His Majesty's Ambassador.'[1]

As at the time the military delegations were leaving London the question of definition of aggression was still hanging in the air, the British Government considered that there was no need for haste in their dispatch.

Here there once again was revealed the divergence between London and Paris. In a telegram of August 13 Seeds asked Halifax to resolve his perplexities.

'Admiral Drax's written instructions', wrote Seeds, 'seem to be to the effect that military conversations must go slowly until agreement has been reached on political questions still outstanding. . . . On the other hand, the French General has instructions to do his utmost to conclude military agreement at the earliest possible date, and such instructions clearly do not tally with those given to Admiral Drax.'

Yes, of course, there was an obvious divergence between

1. *Documents on British Foreign Policy, 1919–1939*, Third Series, Vol. VI, p. 763.

London and Paris on this point. And not only between London
and Paris, but also (and this was particularly significant) between
the British Government in London and its own Ambassador in
Moscow. However well trained Seeds might be, even he in the end
could not stand the British Government's mockery of the interests
of European security and of the most elementary common sense.
In the same telegram, Seeds went on:

'I shall be grateful for earliest possible information as to
whether His Majesty's Government definitely wish progress of
military talks, beyond vague generalities, to be made dependent
on a previous solution of "indirect aggression" problem. I should
deeply regret if that were the actual decision of His Majesty's
Government, as all indications so far go to show that Soviet
military negotiators are really out for business.'[1]

Could the political short-sightedness of the then leaders of the
British bourgeoisie be more blatant, blinded as they were by their
class prejudice?

*   *   *

At this point, in substance, end my personal recollections of
the tripartite negotiations of 1939, because after the departure of
the military delegations to the U.S.S.R. these negotiations ceased,
so far as London was concerned. Their centre of gravity put on
military uniform and moved to Moscow, where I took no direct
part in them. However, I cannot simply put a full stop here. The
logic of the whole narrative impels me to describe, if only briefly,
what took place in Moscow and how the lamentable story of the
tripartite negotiations ended. In this part of my exposition I will
have to make use not of my own recollections but of what I heard
from other reliable witnesses of the events in Moscow, and what I
learned later on from various printed and documentary sources.

1. *Documents on British Foreign Policy, 1919–1939*, Third Series, Vol.
VI, pp. 682–3.

7

Military negotiations in Moscow

IN CONTRAST to the British and French governments, the Soviet Government treated the forthcoming military negotiations with all the seriousness which they deserved.

The Soviet mission consisted of persons of the very first rank. Marshal K. E. Voroshilov, at that time People's Commissar for Defence of the U.S.S.R., was appointed head of the mission. Its members consisted of Army Commander Grade I, and Chief of the General Staff, B. M. Shaposhnikov; the People's Commissar for the Navy, Flagman of the Fleet Grade II, N. G. Kuznetsov, the Chief of the Air Force, Army Commander Grade II, A. D. Loktionov; and the Deputy Chief of the General Staff, Corps Commander I. V. Smorodinov.

The British and French missions, on their arrival in Leningrad, were met by the highest representatives of the military and naval authorities in that city. They were taken on a sight-seeing tour of Leningrad and its environs. Sir William Seeds, in his report to the Foreign Office, underlined that the Soviet authorities 'were evidently anxious to place every facility at their disposal'.[1]

In Moscow the British and French delegations also had a first-class reception, and on the very day of their arrival were received by the People's Commissar for Foreign Affairs and the People's Commissar for Defence; while in the evening they attended a dinner organized in their honour by the Soviet mission at the Spiridonovka House for official receptions. Describing his visit to K. E. Voroshilov, Seeds remarked in the same report:

1. *Documents on British Foreign Policy, 1919–1939*, Third Series, Vol. VII, p. 45.

'Marshal Voroshilov, whom I had not had an opportunity of meeting before, wore an unusually smart white summer uniform and gave a most favourable impression, both of friendliness and energy. He seemed really pleased to meet the mission.'[1]

The dinner at the Spiridonovka made a deep impression on the British Ambassador.

'The reception lasted until a late hour—the dinner being followed by an excellent concert', he wrote in his report. 'A cordial atmosphere prevailed, though language difficulties were somewhat of a hindrance to conversation. In an official statement which appeared in *Izvestia* of August 12 reference was made to the "friendly toasts" that were exchanged at the dinner.'[2]

In this way the Soviet side did everything possible to show its serious attitude to the negotiations for a military convention, and its sincerity in the desire to create an effective barrier against any repetition of aggression. The British themselves bore witness to this. But what of the Anglo-French side? Alas, here everything remained as before: the sabotage of a triple pact continued.

This was revealed at the very first official meeting of the three missions on August 12. After all the formalities had been completed the head of the Soviet delegation proposed that they should familiarize themselves with the written powers which each delegation possessed. With this he presented the written powers of the Soviet delegation, which declared that our delegation was empowered 'to conduct negotiations with the British and French military missions and sign a military convention on questions pertaining to the organization of the military defence of Britain, France and the U.S.S.R. against aggression in Europe.'[3]

General Doumenc, the head of the French delegation, read his powers, which authorized him 'to come to an agreement with the

1. Ibid., p. 46.

2. Ibid., pp. 46–7.

3. 'Negotiations between the military missions of the U.S.S.R., Britain and France in Moscow in August, 1939' (referred to henceforth as 'Negotiations . . .'), published in the Soviet magazine *International Affairs*, February, 1959, p. 145.

Supreme Command of the Soviet Armed Forces on all questions pertaining to co-operation between the armed forces of the two countries.'[1] This was considerably less than the authority given to the Soviet delegation, but nevertheless General Doumenc was able to conduct serious negotiations with the Soviet side.

The position of Admiral Drax turned out to be much worse. It transpired that he had no written authority at all! Could there have been a better proof of the lack of seriousness with which the British Government approached the military negotiations? It was clear that the British mission had been sent to Moscow not in order urgently to conclude a military convention but to carry on irresponsible conversations about a military convention. Admiral Drax attempted to get out of his difficult situation by saying that if it were convenient to transfer the negotiations to London, he would be given full powers: but the head of the Soviet delegation remarked amid general laughter that 'bringing papers from London to Moscow was easier than for so big a company to go to London'.[1] In the end the Admiral promised to ask his Government for written powers—which he received only on August 21 when, as we shall see later, the need for them had disappeared.

Thus the lack of written authority for Admiral Drax was the last drop which filled the cup of the Soviet Government's patience, that had lasted for so many months. It became finally convinced that Chamberlain was incorrigible and that the hope of a pact had become an infinitely small quantity. The problem of defending Soviet interests would have to be solved otherwise. However, it would be politically unwise sharply to break off negotiations, so long as the other side had not renounced them.

In spite of the absence of properly drawn-up authority for Admiral Drax, the Soviet delegation said it did not object to the conference continuing. And, in fact, on August 13, 14, 15, 16 and 17 seven meetings were held, at which the three sides exchanged information about their armed forces and their plans in the event of Hitlerite aggression. Admiral Drax, Air Marshal Burnett and

1. Ibid., p. 145
1. Ibid., p. 145

General Heywood spoke on behalf of Britain, Generals Doumenc and Valin and Captain Willaume for France, and Army Commander Shaposhnikov, Army Commander Loktionov and People's Commissar for the Navy Kuznetsov took part in the discussion for the U.S.S.R.

The general picture of the armed forces of the three Powers proved to be the following:

France disposed of 110 divisions, without reckoning its anti-aircraft forces, its coastal defence forces and its troops in Africa. In addition there were about 200,000 soldiers of Republican Spain (a figure which was much exaggerated), who had taken refuge in France after the victory of Franco and had asked to be incorporated in the French forces. The French Army possessed 4,000 modern tanks and 3,000 large-calibre guns of 150 mm. and higher (without reckoning divisional artillery). The French Air Force consisted of 2,000 first-line aircraft, of which about two-thirds were modern as then understood—namely, aircraft with a speed of 450–500 km. per hour in the case of fighters and 400–450 km. in the case of bombers.

Britain had ready six divisions, could 'in the shortest possible time' transfer another 10 to the Continent, and 'in the second echelon' add another sixteen divisions—in all, therefore, thirty-two divisions. The air forces of Great Britain comprised more than 3,000 first-line aircraft.

The Soviet Union possessed to fight aggression in Europe 120 infantry and sixteen cavalry divisions, 5,000 heavy guns, 9,000 to 10,000 tanks and 5,000 to 5,500 fighting aircraft.

In addition the three Great Powers possessed navies among which the British was particularly powerful.[1]

It will be seen that the armed forces of the anticipated signatories of the triple pact were very impressive, and far surpassed the then forces of Germany and Italy. These forces would unquestionably have been sufficient to avert Fascist aggression, but only on one condition—if all three governments really wanted to

1. 'Negotiations . . .' (*International Affairs*, 1959, February, pp. 144–58; March, pp. 139–58).

set up a single effective front against Hitler and Mussolini. The Soviet Government wanted that very much, but this could not in the least be said of the governments of France and, particularly, Britain. Here are two characteristic facts.

At the meeting of August 14 there took place the following exchange of opinion between Marshal Voroshilov and General Doumenc:

VOROSHILOV: Yesterday I asked General Doumenc the following question: what part do the present missions, or the General Staffs of France and Britain, consider the Soviet Union should play in war against an aggressor, if he attacks France and Britain, if he attacks Poland or Rumania, or Poland and Rumania together, and if he attacks Turkey?

GENERAL DOUMENC: General Gamelin holds the view, and I as his subordinate share it, that our initial task is for each party to hold firm on its own front and group all its forces on that front. As regards the countries referred to earlier, we consider that it is their duty to defend their own territory. But we extend help to them when they ask for it.

VOROSHILOV: But what if they do not ask for it?

DOUMENC: We know that they are in need of assistance.

VOROSHILOV: If they do not ask for this assistance in good time it will mean that they have put up their hands, that they have surrendered.

DOUMENC: That would be highly deplorable.

VOROSHILOV: What will the French Army do then?

DOUMENC: France will then keep on her own front the forces she deems necessary.[1]

And so the French General Staff was obviously suffering from a passivity complex. In the event of a new 'leap' by Hitler, it was recommending the future participants in the pact each to 'hold firm on its own front' and to wait . . . to wait until the victim of aggression appealed for their assistance. Applied to the U.S.S.R., this meant that, should Hitler attack Poland or Rumania, the Soviet Government should concentrate its forces on its western

1. 'Negotiations . . .' (*International Affairs*, February, 1959, p. 154.

frontier and calmly observe what was happening on the other side. Only if the Polish or Rumanian governments requested, should it come to their assistance. . . . And if they did not make the request? Or if they asked too late? What then? . . . It could not be doubted that the strategy which the French General Staff was recommending could lead only to the triumph of the aggressor.

Even more acute was the divergence between the Soviet side and the Anglo-French side which revealed itself on another question. The Soviet side considered that, if one were seriously thinking about plans for fighting the aggressors, it was necessary beforehand to come to a precise agreement as to the practical action to be taken at the moment of danger, without waiting for the critical moment to arrive. It was for this reason that at the same meeting of August 14 the head of the Soviet delegation, bearing in mind that the U.S.S.R. and Germany had no common frontier, put the direct question to the heads of the British and French missions:

'Do the French and British General Staffs think that the Soviet land forces will be admitted to Polish territory in order to make direct contact with the enemy in case Poland is attacked? . . . Is it proposed to allow Soviet troops across Rumanian territory if the aggressor attacks Rumania?'

Having made clear later that it was a question first of all of passage of Soviet troops through the Vilno Corridor and Galicia, the Soviet representative underlined that 'if this question is not solved favourably I doubt the usefulness of our conversations'.[1]

What did the British and French missions reply?

At first they began to argue that there was no problem of passage of Soviet troops at all since, in the words of General Doumenc, in the event of an attack by Germany 'Poland and Rumania will implore you, Marshal, to come to their assistance'. When, however, Marshal Voroshilov retorted that 'perhaps they will not',[2] Drax and Doumenc gave him to understand that the question put by the Soviet side was a political question, beyond

1. Ibid., pp. 155–6.
2. Ibid., p. 156.

the competence of the military missions. But as the head of the Soviet delegation stated that the question of the passage of Soviet troops was 'most cardinal', and that without its satisfactory solution there could be no question of concluding a military convention, the heads of the two western delegations in a written communication declared that a reply to the question put by the Soviet side required an approach to the governments of Poland and Rumania. They recommended the Government of the U.S.S.R. to do this, and at the same time allowed that the appropriate question could be put by London and Paris.

The Soviet Government, of course, had no grounds for making *démarches* in Warsaw and Bucharest. As a result, Drax and Doumenc undertook to ask the British and French governments to secure a reply from Poland and Rumania to the question of the passage of Soviet troops.

At the end of that same session on August 14 the Soviet side read a written statement which declared, among other things:

'The Soviet military mission expresses its regret at the absence of an exact answer on the part of the British and French missions to the question raised about the right of passage of Soviet armed forces over Polish and Rumanian territory.

'The Soviet military mission considers that without a positive solution of this question the whole present attempt to conclude a military convention between France, Britain and the Soviet Union is, in its opinion, doomed to failure.'[1]

The following day, August 15, Drax stated that both missions had sent enquiries to London and Paris respectively on the question which interested the Soviet delegation. But as, however, there were no replies from London and Paris either on the 16th or the 17th, the Soviet side stated that 'if there is no reply today and tomorrow from the British and French governments we shall, unfortunately, have to interrupt our meetings for some time while we wait for it.'[2]

1. Ibid., p. 158.
2. 'Negotiations . . .' (*International Affairs*, 1959, No. 3, p. 153.)

As a result it was agreed that the next meeting of the delegations would take place on August 21.

However, the people in Paris and London who were continuing the tactics of sabotage were obviously not in a hurry. Neither on the 18th or the 19th, nor on the 20th or the 21st did the British and French missions receive any reply to their enquiry. In view of this, on the evening before the appointed day, Drax and Doumenc sent Voroshilov a letter asking that the meeting be postponed another three or four days. The head of the Soviet delegation did not agree to this proposal, and a meeting took place after all on the morning of August 21. Here Marshal Voroshilov firmly stated that in view of the delay in replies to the cardinal question of the negotiations it was necessary to arrange a longer interruption, since members of the Soviet delegation would now be engaged in the autumn manœuvres.

Understanding that things looked like a collapse of the negotiations, Drax, on behalf of both delegations, made an attempt to throw responsibility for this failure on the Soviet Government. In the written statement which he read they asserted:

'We were invited here to negotiate a convention for military action. We therefore find it difficult to understand the action of the Soviet mission, whose intention it apparently was to start out by raising difficult and important political questions. . . . The French and British missions are therefore unable to accept any responsibility for the delays that have arisen.'[1]

At the afternoon session on the same day the Soviet side likewise read out the written reply of the Soviet mission, from which I quote the following extracts:

'Just as British and American troops in the last world war could not have taken part in the general action with the military forces of France had they not had the opportunity of operating on French soil, similarly the Soviet armed forces cannot co-operate with the armed forces of Britain and France if they are not allowed on Polish and Rumanian territory. That is a military axiom. . . .

'The Soviet military mission cannot picture to itself how the

1. Ibid., p. 156.

governments and General Staffs of Britain and France, in sending their missions to the U.S.S.R. for discussions on a military convention, could have failed to give them precise and positive instructions on such an elementary question. . . .

'If, however, this axiomatic question is turned by the British and French into a great problem requiring long study this means that there is every reason to doubt their desire for effective and serious military co-operation with the U.S.S.R.

'In view of the above, the responsibility for the delay in the military negotiations and for the interruption in these conversations naturally falls on the British and French sides.'[1]

In this way, thanks to the sabotage of the British and French governments, the military negotiations likewise found themselves in a blind alley.

1. Ibid., p. 157.

M

8

The Soviet Government's dilemma

WHAT was to be done?

There arose before the Soviet Government an acute dilemma. Should it continue tripartite negotiations with the governments of Britain and France, which obviously did not desire a pact; or should it seek for other ways to strengthen its security?

At this point one could not help recalling a striking episode in the early history of the Soviet Union.

Immediately after the October Revolution the young and still weak Soviet State was faced with the solution of an important and difficult problem: how to end the war in the midst of which it had been born? On the solution of this problem depended the whole future of the revolution and of the Soviet country, and, more than that, of all humanity.

What was the situation in fact? The great revolution in Russia had only just taken place. It had encountered furious resistance from the old ruling classes, supported by the whole capitalist world. It had inherited from the Tsarist régime terrible economic collapse and illiteracy among wide masses of the people. In order to maintain itself and live out these difficulties the young and still weak Soviet Republic needed most of all peace, or at any rate a temporary 'breathing space'.

How did the Soviet Government under Lenin's leadership then act?

In the famous Decree on Peace of November 8, 1917, and in the subsequent Notes addressed to the various governments, it appealed first of all to all the belligerent countries, proposing that they immediately cease hostilities and conclude a general, just and democratic peace without annexations or indemnities. The Soviet Government considered that such a termination of the war was the most desirable, and most in keeping with the interests of the working class and all mankind.

It is well known that the Soviet Government's initiative fell on stony ground. Neither Germany and Austria-Hungary, nor Britain, France and the U.S.A. responded to the appeal of the Soviet State. Locked in deadly combat, they continued the war for more than another year.

How did the Soviet Government and Lenin act in this situation?

The Soviet Government did not take the path of 'revolutionary war' to which the so-called 'Left Communists' were pushing it, nor the path of 'neither peace nor war' which was recommended by Trotsky. The Soviet Government chose another way. The course of argument was the following: if for reasons over which it had no control it could not at present secure a general democratic peace, which would of course have been the best way out, at least it should ensure that its own country should leave the war as soon as possible. It was exceptionally important to save the revolution and to save the fatherland of Socialism. If a breathing space could not be secured by the conclusion of a general peace it should be secured even through a separate peace with Germany. Yes, of course, Germany was an aggressively imperialist Power—but what of that? Soviet Russia was existing not in a vacuum, but in concrete encirclement by a hostile capitalist world. Since a general democratic peace, in spite of the will of the Soviet Government, could not be achieved at the time, it must seek even a temporary breathing space by agreement with German imperialism (of course on condition that it did not interfere in the internal affairs of Soviet Russia).

And Lenin took the resolute step which then seemed to some renunciation of the principles of the October Revolution, but which in reality was a manœuvre of genius, precisely for the greater glory of those principles.

Hence followed the Peace of Brest-Litovsk—a very painful

peace, a peace with annexations and indemnities at the expense of the Soviet Republic, a bad peace, an 'obscene' peace as Lenin called it. But that peace gave the Soviet Republic what it most of all needed at the time; it provided a breathing space which, as the future was to show, was the necessary preliminary for the powerful development of the U.S.S.R. in later decades. History has completely justified Lenin's action in those difficult days. Lenin showed himself in them as the greatest master of revolutionary action, who would not sacrifice its substance for the sake of a revolutionary phrase.[1]

In 1939, twenty-two years after Brest, the Soviet Government once again was faced with an important and difficult problem. Of course much had changed in the world during the intervening years, and particularly in the strength of the Soviet Union, which had grown enormously. But in the situation of 1939 there were nevertheless a number of elements similar to those which dominated in 1917.

In 1939 the Soviet Union was again threatened with a great danger —the danger of aggression by the Fascist Powers, particularly Germany and Japan, and moreover of the creation of a united capitalist front against the Soviet State. For the history of the tripartite negotiations had demonstrated vividly that Chamberlain and Daladier might at any moment go over to the side of the Fascist Powers and, in one form or another, support their attack on the U.S.S.R. This danger had to be covered at all costs —but how?

The very best way, for which the Soviet Government had been

1 An interesting confirmation of the correctness of Lenin's manœuvring in the days of Brest—confirmation, strange to say, from the camp of our enemies—are the meditations of the German General Hoffmann, who took part in the Brest-Litovsk negotiations on the German side. In his book *The War of Lost Opportunities* he wrote: 'I have often wondered whether it would not have been better for the Imperial Government and the Supreme War Command to have avoided any negotiations with the Bolshevist authorities. By the very fact that we gave them the possibility of concluding peace, and thus meeting the passionate desire of the masses of the people, we helped them to seize power firmly and maintain it.'

striving with all the strength and all the resources at its command, would have been the creation of a mighty defensive coalition of Powers who were not interested in launching a second world war. In practice, what was involved in the first instance was a triple pact of mutual assistance between Britain, France and the U.S.S.R. It has been demonstrated sufficiently in the preceding pages that the Soviet Government first took precisely this road. It was the Soviet Government which proposed to Britain and France the conclusion of a triple pact of mutual assistance, it was the Soviet Government which for four whole months stubbornly negotiated with London and Paris for such a pact, displaying almost angelic patience in the course of the negotiations.

But as a result of the consistent sabotage of Chamberlain and Daladier, who banked on provoking a German-Soviet war, the tripartite negotiations in August, 1939, finally reached an impasse, and the argument about the passage of Soviet troops through the territory of Poland and Rumania was but the final and decisive link in the long chain of previous disappointments. Now it became perfectly clear that, through no fault of our own, a triple pact for combating the aggressors was impracticable. For in reality, even if we had admitted the possibility that such a pact might be signed in the long run, the question arose first of all, how much longer would be needed to achieve such a result? And would it not come too late to arrest the raised hand of the aggressors? After all, the soil of Europe was already aflame! And then arose a still more important question. How would Britain and France observe the pact which they had signed? We had recently witnessed the lamentable examples of Austria, Czechoslovakia and Spain. The British and French governments had simply betrayed these countries. Where was the guarantee that they would behave any better in fulfilling their obligations towards the U.S.S.R.? Was it not much more probable that Chamberlain and Daladier at the critical moment would, on one pretext or another, turn their backs on us? Every justification for these doubts was confirmed three weeks later when Germany attacked Poland.

There was in fact no ground for reckoning on an effective triple pact now, in August, 1939. Was it worth while, in that case, continuing the tripartite negotiations? Was it worth while supporting illusions among the masses as to the possibility of a defensive alliance of Britain, France and the U.S.S.R. against the Fascist aggressors? Of course it was not.

Something else had to be thought of. And here the manœuvres of Lenin in the days of Brest provided the reply to the question of what should be done.

In the event of the conversations with Britain and France coming to an end, two possible prospects appeared before the Soviet Government—a policy of isolation, or agreement with Germany. But in the circumstances of that moment, when the guns were already going off on our Far Eastern frontiers (at Lake Hassan and Khalkhin-Gol), when Chamberlain and Daladier were making great efforts to incite Germany against the U.S.S.R., and when in Germany itself there was hesitation as to the direction in which the first blow should be struck—in such a situation a policy of isolation would have been extremely perilous, and the Soviet Government with full justification rejected it. There remained one way out—agreement with Germany. Was it feasible? Yes, it was, for from the very beginning of the tripartite negotiations Berlin had been extremely nervous, and had followed all their twists and turns with great attention.

As has already been pointed out, politicians and historians in the west have created the legend that in the spring and summer of 1939 the U.S.S.R. was carrying on a double game. Thus, for example, Daladier wrote in April, 1946: 'Since the month of May the U.S.S.R. had conducted two negotiations, one with France, the other with Germany.'[1] Churchill is less definite, but he too remarks in his war memoirs: 'It is not even now possible to fix the moment when Stalin definitely abandoned all intention of working with the Western Democracies and of coming to terms with Hitler.'[2] Hence it follows that Churchill likewise admits the

1. Quoted by Winston Churchill, *The Second World War*, Vol. I (1948), p. 289.
2. Ibid., p. 284.

possibility that the Soviet Government was conducting a double game.

In order to prove the existence of such a double game, the American Government in 1949 published a special volume on Soviet-German relations in 1939–41, containing an extremely tendentious selection of documents of the German Ministry for Foreign Affairs, seized by the Western Powers as trophies at the end of the second world war.[1]

In view of the foregoing, it is hardly necessary to prove that all such assertions are a slanderous and malignant invention. Nevertheless it is of interest to examine the collection mentioned somewhat more attentively, and to see what the documents it contains narrate. In doing so, two facts must be borne in mind.

First, its compilers were undoubtedly seeking to choose those materials which were most to their advantage, and consequently least to the advantage of the U.S.S.R.

Secondly, the documents it contains consist of correspondence between the German Ministry for Foreign Affairs and its Embassy in Moscow, records of the conversations between German and Soviet diplomats, discussions of the foreign policy of the U.S.S.R., etc.—and all representing only the reflection of the views of one side, the German. Naturally, therefore, the materials in question are entirely anti-Soviet in their tendency, and sometimes are simply a falsification of the truth to the advantage of Germany. If Lord Halifax, as was shown above, could completely distort in his record the substance of my talk with him on June 12, 1939, why should we have greater confidence in the documents of German diplomats?

Thus the collection referred to contains the quintessence of all that can be said *against* the Soviet Union. In any case, there can be found in its pages no indulgences and no understatements favouring the U.S.S.R. It is all the more interesting, therefore, to look at the documents contained in this 'act of accusation' against the Soviet Government. What then do they say?

1. *Nazi–Soviet Relations, 1939–1941*, Department of State, Washington, 1948 (referred to further as 'N.S.R.').

The whole collection is divided into eight sections, of which only the first is of interest for our purposes. It almost entirely covers the period of the tripartite negotiations (from April 17 to August 14, 1939). There are thirty-two documents in this first section, very unequally distributed: one in April, twelve in May, seven in June, five in July, seven up to August 14. However, much more important than their chronological distribution is their content.

In April, May and June the documents in the main deal with economic questions of a current nature. Political questions are also touched upon sometimes, but only infrequently and in passing, bearing the character of entirely noncommittal mutual soundings. Usually it is a question of the possibility of improving relations between the U.S.S.R. and Germany, which at that time were marked by extreme tension. Such conversations are an everyday matter of routine between the diplomatic representatives of any two countries, the relations between which leave much to be desired. There is nothing 'sinister' directed against the interests of Britain and France in the Soviet-German conversations of this period. There can be no talk of any duplicity in Soviet policy. I will give a few concrete examples.

As I have mentioned, there is only one document for April. It is a record of conversations between German and Soviet representatives in Berlin as to the status of the Soviet Trade Delegation in Prague, and as to the fulfilment of Soviet orders placed with the Skoda Works before Czechoslovakia had been seized by Germany. This question, therefore, was in the sphere of current economic relations between the two countries, and had no edge directed against the Western Powers.

On May 5 Schnurre, a prominent official of the German Ministry for Foreign Affairs principally concerned with economic questions, invited Astakhov, the Soviet *chargé d'affaires* in Berlin, to come and see him, and informed him that the Skoda Works had been instructed to fulfil the Soviet orders. Astakhov naturally expressed his satisfaction at this information, and enquired whether the Soviet-German negotiations (also on economic questions) which had been interrupted in February, 1939, might not be renewed in the near future. To this Schnurre gave an evasive reply. Thereupon Schnurre, in his record of the conversation, writes:

'Astakhov touched upon the dismissal of Litvinov [which had taken place two days before—I.M.] and tried without asking direct questions to learn whether this event would cause a change in our position towards the Soviet Union.'[1]

If Schnurre gives a correct account of what Astakhov said in this connection (and of this, of course, one cannot in the least be sure) one must suppose that he was wishing to probe a little. Litvinov's resignation was then being interpreted in the West as meaning that the U.S.S.R. was passing from co-operation with Britain and France to a policy of isolation, or even to one of co-operation with Germany. As I have already mentioned, Halifax on May 6 put me the direct question of how Litvinov's being relieved of the post of People's Commissar for Foreign Affairs was to be understood, and whether the proposals for a triple pact of mutual assistance we had made on April 17 remained in force. It might be useful to the Soviet Government to know how the ruling circles in Germany reacted to the changes which had taken place in Moscow. But it is most probable that in reality the question as to the effect of Litvinov's resignation on German-Soviet relations was put by Schnurre himself, and that it was only in his record of the conversation that he represented matters as though the question had been put by Astakhov (such devices are met with in the practice of bourgeois diplomacy). For, when on May 9, four days later, the same Astakhov presented Filippov, the new Tass correspondent, to an official of the German Ministry for Foreign Affairs, Braun von Stumm, the latter asked what influence on Soviet foreign policy would be exercised by the change in the post of People's Commissar for Foreign Affairs. Astakhov replied that Litvinov carried out a policy which was not his own but which complied 'with general principles'.[2] Whichever version of

1. N.S.R., p. 3.
2. N.S.R., p. 4.

this conversation was the correct one, there can be no doubt in any case that the sounding as to the effect of Litvinov's resignation meant nothing even remotely resembling negotiations for an agreement with Germany.

On May 17 Astakhov again visited Schnurre and talked with him about the status of the Soviet Trade Delegation in Prague. Schnurre then writes in his report:

'During the subsequent conversation Astakhov again referred in great detail to the development of German-Soviet relations.'

It is not clear from Schnurre's way of putting it who was the initiator of this conversation: but even if it was Astakhov, Schnurre's own record shows that all he said on the subject was impregnated with a great distrust of Germany. Astakhov expressed satisfaction at a certain restraint in respect of the U.S.S.R. which the German press had been displaying in the preceding weeks, but added that 'the Soviets could not judge whether this was only a temporary break that was used for tactical reasons'. Astakhov pointed to the example of Italo-Soviet relations as a model of what was also possible in Russo-German relations.[1]

In all the conversations between Soviet representatives in Berlin and German diplomats there was absolutely nothing which went beyond the bounds of natural everyday concern for the improvement of relations between two countries which were in a state of great tension. It would not be possible even with a microscope to find in them any signs of some ill-intentioned 'conspiracy' against Britain and France.

On May 20 there took place a much more important event. On that day Schulenburg, the German Ambassador in Moscow, visited the People's Commissar for Foreign Affairs and made an attempt to revive the German-Soviet trade negotiations which had been suspended in February. This was an obvious advance which Germany was making to the U.S.S.R. But what did he get in reply? The People's Commissar not only did not express any delight at this but on the contrary remarked fairly sharply that the whole history of the previous trade negotiations between the two

1. Ibid., p. 5.

countries was giving the Soviet Government the impression that Germany was playing some frivolous game—a game which was evidently pursuing some political end or other. From this the People's Commissar drew the natural conclusion that before these negotiations were resumed the necessary 'political bases' should be constructed, i.e. that political relations between the two countries should be improved.[1]

Schulenburg's report on this conversation had a very discouraging effect in Berlin, and on May 21 State Secretary Weizsaecker telegraphed to the German Ambassador in Moscow:

'On basis of results so far of your discussions with Molotov, we must now sit tight (*ganz still zu halten*) and wait to see if the Russians will speak more openly.'[2]

Such is the true picture of German-Soviet relations in May, 1939, as is clear even from the documents of the German Ministry for Foreign Affairs, tendentiously selected on the orders of our adversaries in the U.S.A. Yet Daladier dares to allege, without a scrap of evidence, that the U.S.S.R. 'since the month of May had conducted two negotiations, one with France, the other with Germany'!

However, the tripartite negotiations very much worried Hitlerite Germany, and the 'sitting tight' did not last very long. On May 27 Weizsaecker wrote to Schulenburg: 'We are of the opinion here that the English-Russian combination certainly will not be easy to prevent',[3] and on May 30, by Hitler's special instruction, he invited Astakhov to come and see him, and declared that the status of the Soviet Trade Delegation in Prague involved great problems of principle. He therefore put before Astakhov at full length the question of political relations between Germany and the U.S.S.R. In doing so, Weizsaecker developed the following conception. In Berlin, Communism was not liked, and they had put an end to it in the country. They did not expect in Berlin that there would be any liking for National-Socialism in

1. N.S.R., p. 6.
2. Ibid., p. 7.
3. Ibid., p. 9.

Moscow. But ideological differences should not interfere with the maintainance of normal business relations between the two countries.

This was a new German advance to the U.S.S.R.: but Astakhov reacted to it very cautiously. From Weiszaecker's record it is clear that he reminded the latter of the distrust of Hitlerite Germany which had become rooted in Moscow, but of course agreed with Weizsaecker's view that, in spite of ideological differences, it was quite possible for the two countries to normalize their relations. Such, after all, was one of the fundamental principles of Soviet foreign policy in general.

Even more important was the fact that Moscow did not react in any way to this new step in the German diplomatic offensive. During June very animated negotiations on trade affairs went on between Germany and the U.S.S.R., but by the end of the month they had ceased, because of the impossibility of settling the differences existing between the two sides. The U.S.S.R. considered the German position insufficiently favourable towards itself.

In spite of this reverse, and in spite of the fact that the Soviet Government had not responded to the conversation between Weizsaecker and Astakhov on May 30, Schulenburg on June 28 visited the People's Commissar for Foreign Affairs and once again, on behalf of his Government, officially declared that Germany desired normalization of the relations between the two countries. In doing so he pointed to a number of facts (the conclusion by Germany of pacts of non-aggression with the Baltic States, a change in the tone of the German press towards the U.S.S.R., etc.) which, in his opinion, were evidence that Berlin was ready to meet the point of view of the Soviet Union.

This was in accordance with Soviet wishes, and indicated a change in German policy which was favourable for us. However, the People's Commissar here too displayed no particular enthusiasm but, judging from Schulenburg's own record, calmly replied that he received Schulenburg's words 'with satisfaction' and that 'the foreign policy of the Soviet Government was, in

accordance with the pronouncements of its leaders, aimed at the
cultivation of good relations with all countries, and this, of course,
applied—provided there was reciprocity—to Germany too'.[1]

Thereafter a whole month passed—that same lamentable month
of July in which the British and French governments were
stubbornly sabotaging the integration of the pact and the military
convention—but the collection in question does not provide *one
single document* testifying to any progressive coming together of
the U.S.S.R. and Germany in the political sphere. In spite of that
sabotage, in spite of the growing doubts of the Soviet Government as to the possibility of concluding the triple pact, it firmly
continued its negotiations with Britain and France and abstained
from any advances in the direction of Germany.

Quite otherwise was the behaviour of Berlin. The tripartite
negotiations, and in particular the agreement that British and
French missions should be sent to Moscow, aroused ever-growing
alarm in Hitlerite government circles. They feverishly discussed
and attempted to put into effect various measures which they
thought might frustrate, or at any rate postpone, the signature of
a triple pact. In the second half of July the trade negotiations
between Germany and the U.S.S.R., suspended three weeks
before, were renewed, and this time the German side willingly
advanced towards what the Soviet side desired.

On July 26 Schnurre, by direct instruction from above,
invited Astakhov and the Soviet Trade Representative in Germany, Babarin, to dinner. Here Schnurre zealously sought to
demonstrate that good relations were quite possible between
Germany and the U.S.S.R., and even indicated concretely the
successive stages by which they could be improved. Schnurre
asserted further that Germany was ready for a far-reaching
agreement with the U.S.S.R. on all problems 'from the Baltic to
the Black Sea'.

But what did Schnurre's Soviet guests reply? I quote his own
record:

'With the strong agreement of Babarin, Astakhov designated

1. Ibid., pp. 26–7.

the way of *rapprochement* with Germany as the one that corres-
ponded with the vital interests of the two countries. However, he
emphasized that the tempo must probably be very slow and
gradual. The Soviet Union had been forced to feel itself most
seriously menaced by the National-Socialist foreign policy. . . .
Astakhov mentioned the Anti-Comintern Pact and our relations
with Japan, Munich and the free hand in Eastern Europe that we
gained there, the political consequences of which were bound to
be directed against the Soviet Union. . . . Moscow could not quite
believe in a shift of German policy with respect to the Soviet
Union. A change could only be expected gradually.'[1]

It will be seen that the Soviet representatives in Berlin took a
very cautious attitude to the speeches of the Nazi siren, and in
any case in their statements did not go beyond the bounds of a
quite legitimate desire to promote an improvement in relations
between the two countries. And here is an interesting assessment
of the general position of the Soviet Government in relation to
the German advances, which we find in a telegram of Weizsaecker
to Schulenburg on July 29:

'It would be important for us to know whether the statements
made to Astakhov and Babarin have found any response in
Moscow. If you see the opportunity of arranging a new talk with
Molotov I request that you sound him out in this sense. . . . If it
should develop that Molotov *abandons the reserve thus far maintained by him* you can advance another step in your presentation'
[my italics—I.M.][2]

And so, in the opinion of the German side, the Soviet Government, during the months from April to July inclusive, had not
responded to the overtures in the German diplomatic offensive.

One week later Germany made a new and very important step
towards the U.S.S.R. On August 3, just when the British and
French military missions were making their unhurried preparations for travelling to Moscow, Ribbentrop invited Astakhov to
come and see him and made a very important statement. The fact

1. Ibid., pp. 32–4.
2. Ibid., p. 36.

that the Minister for Foreign Affairs himself received the *chargé d'affaires* indicated in diplomatic terms the extreme urgency and importance of the *démarche*. Ribbentrop stated that a radical remoulding of German-Soviet relations was possible on two main conditions: (a) non-interference in each other's internal affairs: (b) abandonment [by the U.S.S.R.—I.M.] of a policy directed against German interests. Ribbentrop assured Astakhov that the German Government was favourably disposed towards Moscow and added that if Moscow would meet the German Government in this, then 'there was no problem from the Baltic to the Black Sea that could not be solved between the two of us'.

Astakhov, even in Ribbentrop's record, remained very cautious in his replies, did not commit himself in any way and only stated that 'he thought his Government had the desire to pursue a policy of mutual understanding with Germany'. This, of course, did not in any way contradict the possible conclusion of the triple pact.

Informing Schulenburg of his conversation with Astakhov, Ribbentrop added for the Ambassador himself:

'The *chargé*, who seemed interested, tried several times to pin the conversation down to more concrete terms, whereupon I gave him to understand that I would be prepared to make it more concrete as soon as the Soviet Government officially communicated its fundamental desire for a new relationship: should Astakhov be instructed in this sense, we for our part would be interested in an early definite settlement.'[1]

The next day, August 4, Schulenburg on Ribbentrop's instructions set forth to the People's Commissar for Foreign Affairs all that Ribbentrop had told Astakhov the previous day. And how did the People's Commissar react to the words of the German Ambassador?

Schulenburg informed Berlin that the People's Commissar stated that the Soviet Government was favourably inclined to the conclusion of an economic agreement between the two countries, expressed the opinion that the press on both sides must abstain

1. N.S.R., pp. 37–9.

from anything that might exacerbate relations between them and considered the gradual resumption of cultural relations desirable. Schulenburg went on:

'Going on to the question of political relations, Molotov declared that the Soviet Government also desired normalization and improvement of mutual relations. It was not its fault that relations had so deteriorated. The reason for this he saw, first, in the conclusion of the Anti-Comintern Pact, and in everything that had been said and done in this connection.'

Schulenburg touched on the question of Poland. He said that Germany was striving to settle its differences with Poland by peaceful means. But if it were forced to act otherwise it would take Soviet interests into account. The People's Commissar replied that a peaceful solution between Poland and Germany depended first of all on Germany. As can be seen from Schulenburg's further remarks, this reply did not please him at all.

The German Ambassador did not fail to touch on the tripartite negotiations, to which the People's Commissar replied that they aimed at purely defensive ends.

Commenting on this conversation, Schulenburg wrote to Berlin that his overall impression was that 'the Soviet Government was in fact more prepared for improvement in German-Soviet relations, but that the old mistrust of Germany persists'.[1]

We see, therefore, that throughout the spring and summer of 1939 the Soviet Government maintained complete loyalty towards its western partners in the negotiations. There were no secret conspiracies with Germany directed against them. There were no Soviet attempts to enter into a bloc with Berlin behind Britain's back and to betray London and Paris. There was nothing even remotely resembling Horace Wilson's talks with Wohlthat. German-Soviet relations right up to August bore the character of ordinary diplomatic contacts, coloured moreover by a not too friendly tone. The conversations between the representatives of the two governments were customary conversations, such as are conducted daily by Ministers and Ambassadors on various current

1. N.S.R., pp. 40–1.

questions in all quarters of the globe. Such is the indubitable evidence of those same documents which our adversaries in the United States collected for the express purpose of discrediting the Soviet Government.[1]

Only in August, when the tripartite negotiations as a result of Anglo-French sabotage had finally entered their impasse, when all hope of the conclusion of an effective mutual assistance pact between the U.S.S.R., Britain and France had disappeared, was the Soviet Government obliged to make a major change in its policy. Surely this is a natural and legitimate conclusion when a government discovers that due to special circumstances it has no other choice. Thus in the spring and summer of 1939 there was no double game by the Soviet Government, as its foreign enemies charge, but there was a clear, firm and absolutely loyal striving, in respect of Britain and France, to conclude a triple pact with them against the aggressors. If this proved unattainable in the end the blame should not in any case fall on the U.S.S.R.

However, even now the Soviet Government did not wish to break down all the bridges immediately. On August 3 Germany (precisely Germany, and not the Soviet Union) officially made its far-reaching proposals for a radical reconstruction of relations between the two countries. This reconstruction, first of all, was to normalize those relations, and then was gradually to lead to what in diplomatic language is called friendship. Such a prospect was

1. Here is an interesting piece of evidence, showing the absence of any disloyal acts by the Soviet Government, which comes from sources far from friendly to us. William C. Bullitt, the American Ambassador in Paris, reporting on June 28, 1939, his conversation with the French Premier Daladier, wrote: 'Daladier said that he of course knew he could not trust any Russian assurances [about loyalty in respect of the British and French— I.M.], but that neither the French nor British Embassies nor Secret Services had been able to unearth any information indicating that the Russians were negotiating with the Germans' (*Foreign Relations of the United States, 1939*, Vol. I (Washington, 1956), p. 278). The explanation was simple: there had not been any such negotiations. How are these statements by Daladier to be reconciled with the assertions of the same Daladier, quoted above, alleging that the U.S.S.R. had 'conducted negotiations since the month of May' with Germany behind the back of France?

N

fully in keeping with the peaceable aspirations of the Soviet Government, and its achievement would considerably strengthen the security of the Soviet Union. But Moscow even now did not yield to the seductive picture put before it by Berlin. Moscow continued to think of a triple pact, and wanted to make one final effort to realize the optimum alternative for combating aggression. Notwithstanding each and every doubt born of the preceding history of the tripartite negotiations, Moscow still did not lose hope that perhaps the governments of Britain and France, even though it were five minutes before catastrophe, would have second thoughts and take the correct road.

For that reason Moscow waited another ten days. But Berlin meanwhile could not stand the delay, and tried somehow to hasten the course of events. On August 10, a week after Ribbentrop's conversation with Astakhov, Schnurre, in conversation with the latter, was insisting on the speediest possible clarification of the attitude of the U.S.S.R. to the proposals made to it by the German side.

But Moscow even now continued to abstain from taking a final decision, as it had done ever since Ribbentrop's talk with Astakhov on August 3. Moscow waited while the British and French military missions were sailing on their passenger and cargo steamer from London to Leningrad. It waited while the first consultations were going on with the military missions in the Soviet capital. But when, in the course of these consultations, there arose the question of the passage of Soviet troops through the territories of Poland and Rumania (the central question of any military agreement), when it transpired that neither the British and French military missions nor the British and French governments had any reply to make to this question, when London and Paris reacted to the telegrams sent on this subject by only a protracted silence, Soviet long-suffering patience came to an end. It had become quite clear that Chamberlain and Daladier were incorrigible, and that no collective security for peace-loving Powers could be built with their assistance.

The best method of resisting Fascist aggression had failed,

solely by the fault of Chamberlain and Daladier. The time had come to go over to the only way out which still remained.

The position of the Soviet Government during the tripartite negotiations could be compared to the position of a man who is being overtaken by the incoming tide: another moment, and his head will disappear under the waters, if he does not make some rapid and resolute effort to reach a rock which the tide will not submerge.

In fact, the danger of a second world war was coming closer and closer. In March and April it was only noticeable, in May and June it began to assume more definite outlines; in July it clouded the whole atmosphere of Europe, and by the middle of August no one doubted any longer that in a few days' time the guns would begin to speak and aircraft drop their bombs.

It was impossible to wait any longer. Only now, in the middle of August, was the Soviet Government obliged to take its final decision as to what was to be done. The dilemma with which it had previously been faced was now transformed into the bitter necessity of coming to agreement with Germany. The five months' sabotage of the tripartite negotiations by the governments of Britain and France, supported by the U.S.A., left no other way out for the U.S.S.R.

9

The collapse of the tripartite negotiations
and the forced agreement with Germany

On August 14 Schnurre telegraphed to Schulenburg that he
had been visited by Astakhov and told that the Soviet Government was ready for 'a discussion on the individual groups of
questions' in the sphere of German-Soviet relations. The Soviet
Government proposed that the negotiations should be carried on
in Moscow.[1]

On the same day, August 14, immediately after this communication, Ribbentrop sent Schulenburg an urgent directive to call
on the People's Commissar for Foreign Affairs and state on behalf
of the German Government that 'there exist no real conflicts of
interest between Germany and the U.S.S.R.', that 'there is lacking
all cause for an aggressive attitude on the part of one country
against the other' and that, in the opinion of the German Government, 'there is no question between the Baltic and the Black Seas
which cannot be settled to the complete satisfaction of both
countries'. Ribbentrop underlined the possibility of expanding
German-Soviet economic relations in every direction. Ribbentrop
also stated that with the object of 'a speedy clarification of Ger-
man-Russian relations' he was ready himself to come to Moscow,
on condition that he would be received by Stalin.[2]

Thus the German Government once again took the initiative
and now quite officially made a decisive step forward. On August
15 Schulenburg carried out the instructions he had received from

1. N.S.R., p. 48.
2. Ibid., pp. 50–2.

Berlin. The People's Commissar, as the Ambassador reported to Berlin, 'welcomed German intentions of improving relations with the Soviet Union', but expressed the opinion that Ribbentrop's visit to Moscow 'required adequate preparation'. He was also interested to know whether the German Government was disposed to conclude a pact of non-aggression with the U.S.S.R., sign jointly with the U.S.S.R. a guarantee of the Baltic States and influence Japan for the purpose of improving Soviet-Japanese relations.[1]

On the following day, August 16, Ribbentrop, in a telegram to Schulenburg, asked him urgently to inform the People's Commissar for Foreign Affairs that Germany agreed to conclude a pact of non-aggression with the U.S.S.R., to guarantee the Baltic States jointly with the Soviet Union and to exercise its influence with Japan for an improvement of Japanese-Soviet relations. At the same time he urgently repeated that it was necessary for him to come to Moscow, and stated that he was ready to undertake this journey 'at any time after Friday, August 18'.[2]

On August 18 Schulenburg informed the Soviet Government of all this, and received the Soviet reply to the German proposals of August 14. What was the nature of this reply?

It bore a strictly practical character. It enumerated the reasons which had hitherto obliged the Soviet Government to be suspicious of the intentions of Germany, and to take steps to strengthen the defensive measures of the U.S.S.R., and also to take part in organizing the united front against aggression.

The reply further stated that if the German Government sincerely intended to improve its political relations with the U.S.S.R. the Soviet Government could look upon such a change only with pleasure and, for its own part, was prepared to alter its policy in the direction of an appreciable improvement in relations with Germany.

The reply stated that the Soviet Government considered an improvement of Soviet-German relations was entirely possible,

1. Ibid., p. 52.
2. Ibid., p. 58.

since the principle of the peaceful coexistence of various political systems side by side represented a long-established principle of the foreign policy of the U.S.S.R.

Going on, finally, to the sphere of practical measures, the reply proposed that first of all a trade and credit agreement should be concluded and then, after a short interval, a pact of non-aggression should be signed. As regard the proposed visit to Moscow of the German Minister for Foreign Affairs, the reply stated that the Soviet Government welcomed this as evidence of the serious intentions of the German Government. But it considered that such a visit required thorough preparation, and should be accomplished with the minimum of publicity and newspaper sensation.

We see that the Soviet Government, compelled by Chamberlain and Daladier to change the course of its foreign policy, approached the necessary turning point calmly, soberly, coolheadedly, without any excessive haste. The German Government, on the contrary, was extremely nervous and in a great hurry. In a telegram to Schulenburg on August 18 Ribbentrop gave his Ambassador the following instructions:

'This time please conduct conversation [with the People's Commissar for Foreign Affairs—I.M.] . . . pressing emphatically . . . for a rapid realization of my trip and by opposing appropriately any possible new Russian objections.'[1]

Schulenburg carried out the orders of his Minister: but on August 19 had to inform Ribbentrop that the Soviet Government agreed to the latter's visit only a week after publication of the news that a trade and financial agreement had been signed.

Thereupon Germany brought its heaviest artillery into action. On August 20 Hitler sent a message to Stalin. He stated that the new trade and financial agreement had been signed the day before,[2] and insistently begged him to receive Ribbentrop in

1. Ibid, p. 63.
2. On August 19 there had been signed in Berlin a trade and credit agreement between the U.S.S.R. and Germany, providing for a credit from Germany to the U.S.S.R. of 200,000,000 German marks, for a period of

Moscow not later than August 22 or 23.[3]

The hour of great decision had come for the Soviet Government. Up to now there had been only an exchange of opinions between Moscow and Berlin, mutual probing, the study of each other's frame of mind—but now the question was of concluding a pact of non-aggression itself. It became necessary once again to assess the situation created in the sphere of the tripartite negotiations. Here all was very gloomy, as before. On August 16 Marshal Voroshilov, in reply to General Doumenc's proposal that they should begin drafting a military convention, categorically declared: 'The time has not yet arrived to prepare any document. We have not solved what is for the Soviet side the cardinal problem, that is, the problem of the right of passage for the Soviet armed forces on Polish and Rumanian territory for joint action by the contracting parties against the common enemy.'[4]

The enquiry by the military missions as to the passage of Soviet forces through Poland and Rumania had been sent to London and Paris on August 14. It was now August 21. Seven days had passed, yet there was no reply from the British and French governments. In the feverish atmosphere of the time this prolonged silence was a reply in itself. At the same time the most discouraging information was coming from Warsaw: the 'Government of Colonels' would not at any price permit the passage of Soviet troops through its territory.

In such circumstances there was nothing left for the Soviet Government to do but to take the final and decisive step.

On that same day, August 21, when it was established that London and Paris had not replied for a whole week to the

seven years, at 5 per cent per annum. German goods on account of this credit were to be purchased within two years. Within the same period the U.S.S.R. was to supply Germany with goods to a sum of 180,000,000 marks. It will be seen that the amount covered by the agreement was fairly modest, and could not be compared in any way with the sums of £500,000,000 to £1,000,000,000 which figured as a possible loan in the negotiations of Wohlthat with Hudson and Sir Horace Wilson.

3. N.W.R., p. 66–7.
4. 'Negotiations . . .' (*International Affairs*, 1959, No. 3, p. 148).

enquiry of the military missions, and Marshal Voroshilov in consequence proposed the interruption of the sessions of the military missions, J. V. Stalin gave his reply to Hitler's message. He expressed the hope that the German-Soviet pact of non-aggression would be a turning point for the better in the political relations between the two countries, and agreed that Ribbentrop should come to Moscow on August 23.

As the documents published by the British Government after the war prove, this step by the Soviet Government was more than justified, since it follows from these documents that London did not even intend to give a reply to the enquiry of its own military mission as to the passage of Soviet troops. The sabotage of negotiations for a triple pact continued even at that stage.[1]

On the appointed day Ribbentrop with an appropriate suite flew to Moscow. In the Soviet capital he had two meetings with Stalin. By the end of the same day a Pact of Non-Agression, valid for ten years, had been signed by the U.S.S.R. and Germany. It entered into force immediately upon signature, though its ratification later was provided. The content of the Pact differed little from similar pacts which the U.S.S.R. had concluded in previous years with many other Powers. This was the traditional policy of the Soviet Union, which sought to apply Lenin's principle of peaceful coexistence in practice. The two sides undertook to abstain from any aggression against each other (Article 1), to resolve disputes arising between them only by peaceful means (Article 5), not to participate in any groupings hostile to the other side (Article 4) and not to support any third Power should either side by the object of hostile activities by that third Power (Article 2). Article 3 provided that Germany and the U.S.S.R. would 'remain in contact with each other for the future for consultation, in order to inform each other of questions which affected their common interests'.

I draw attention to the words 'consultation' and 'inform'. Like the whole contents of the Pact, they are unquestionable evidence

1. *Documents on British Foreign Policy, 1919–1939*, Third Series, Vol. VIII, p. 119.

that the document signed on August 23, 1939, was only a Pact of *Non-Aggression*. It was in no way something like a military alliance between the two countries, as western politicians and generals have repeatedly tried to represent it. It did not bind the U.S.S.R. to give any help to Germany whatever. In signing the Pact, the Soviet Government was indulging in no illusions: it presumed that sooner or later Hitler would break the obligations entered into under the Pact. But it considered that the latter gave the U.S.S.R. a certain delay, which would give it the opportunity of making better preparations for a future war. As we know, this delay provided the Soviet Union with nearly two years more of peace.

But the Soviet Government succeeded not only in securing this delay. It also received the assurance from the German Government that hostilities would not be transferred into the Baltic regions. In the situation created by the sabotage of Chamberlain and Daladier on the one hand, and the 'Government of Colonels' in Warsaw on the other, the Soviet Government was in no position to afford the aid to Poland which had been so categorically rejected by the 'Colonels'. All that still could be done was to save Western Ukraine and Western Byelorussia from German invasion. The Soviet Government acted accordingly.

As a result, the U.S.S.R. received the following advantages from the agreement with Germany.

In the first place, the possibility of a united capitalist front against the Soviet Union was averted. More than that, the basis was laid for the formation later on of the anti-Hitler coalition, of which the Western Powers at that moment were not even dreaming.

All that Chamberlain and Daladier were thinking about at that time was at all costs to impel Hitlerite Germany into war with the Soviet Union.

The Pact of Non-Aggression made it impossible to launch the second world war by an attack on the Soviet Union.

The conclusion of the Pact meant the complete bankruptcy of this shameful Munichite strategy.

o

This fact undoubtedly played an important part in the destinies of the Soviet Union, and therefore in the destinies of all mankind.

Secondly, thanks to the agreement with Germany the threat of an attack on the U.S.S.R. by Japan, Germany's ally in the anti-Soviet bloc, disappeared. Had there not been a Pact of Non-Aggression with Germany, the Soviet Union could have found itself in a difficult situation, having to carry on a war on two fronts. For at that moment an attack by Germany on the U.S.S.R. in the west would have meant an attack by Japan in the east. It was precisely in August, 1939, that the battles on the River Khalkhin-Gol reached their greatest intensity, while the Hiranuma Government was stubbornly rejecting a peaceful settlement of the conflict. On the contrary, it was concentrating troops in the Soviet frontier in anticipation of an attack by Germany. But hardly had the German-Soviet Pact of Non-Aggression been signed (August 23) than the Hiranuma Government fell (August 28), and the Abe Government which replaced it hastened to agree to a peaceful settlement of the armed clash. Thus the immediate consequence of the signature of the agreement with Germany was the liquidation of the flames of war which had been blazing up on the Far Eastern frontiers of the U.S.S.R.

Of course, the Soviet Government had to reckon with the fact that its agreement with Germany might be used (and in fact was used) to excite anti-Soviet feelings in the 'democratic' countries, and that people might be found abroad, even among those not hostile to the U.S.S.R., who would not understand its actions correctly (as indeed happened). Nevertheless, considering all the advantages and disadvantages, the Soviet Government came to the conclusion that the pros unquestionably outweighed the cons. As a result, the agreement with Germany was signed. That was the only way out imposed on us by the stupidly criminal policy of Chamberlain and Daladier.

There is one more accusation which the enemies of the Soviet Union abroad like to make. 'By the agreement with Germany', they say, 'you launched the second world war.' Pitiful and blind slanders! As can be seen from all the foregoing, the real responsibility for launching the second world war falls, on the one hand, on Hitler, and on the other on Chamberlain and Daladier (I use these names as symbols). A heavy responsibility for all the miseries caused by the second world war falls on those political groups which in the second half of the thirties were in power in Britain and France: on those groups which in their undiscerning class blindness were carrying on a policy of appeasement of the aggressors, and were hoping for the launching of a war of mutual destruction between Germany and the U.S.S.R. It was just these groups which were setting the trap for the Soviet Union into which, however, they fell themselves—for the first blow of Hitlerite aggression in the second world war fell not on Moscow, but on London and Paris. This was the outcome because Soviet diplomacy proved to be wiser than that of the British and French governments. But for this we have no reason to apologize.

*   *   *

In order to complete my account I have still briefly to tell of the miserable end of the luckless tripartite negotiations of 1939.

On August 22, the day after the final decision of the Soviet Government to make an agreement with Germany, General Doumenc received an urgent communication from Paris. The French Government considered that as soon as Poland was at war with Germany, Soviet troops should have the right to enter Polish territory. The French Government considered. . . . But what did the Polish Government consider? Paris maintained complete silence on such an important question; while from Warsaw there continued to come extremely unfavourable information.

From the documents published by the British Government we now know that Seeds, referring to the instructions received by General Doumenc on August 22, asked London: 'Can we assume that you agree?' But London did not reply to the enquiry of its Moscow Ambassador. Instead, there was written on Seeds'

telegram, in the handwriting of Strang (who had returned home
at the beginning of August): 'It was not possible to send an
answer to this telegram as no decision was taken.'[1] So far did the
sabotage of the British Government go!

At that time we did not know all these details, but we knew the
basic fact that London did not want to reply to the cardinal
question in the military negotiations. This meant a great deal.
And in these circumstances the head of the Soviet delegation
gathered all the three military missions on August 21 and, as was
mentioned earlier, proposed that the meetings should be interrupted. This was simply a diplomatic way of saying that the
tripartite negotiations had suffered a fiasco.

The British and French military missions, like Seeds and
Naggiar, understood the meaning of the Soviet delegation's statement perfectly. And although in the next two, three or four days
the heads of the missions and the Ambassadors of Britain and
France still called upon and talked with the People's Commissars
for Defence and Foreign Affairs, this could no longer change the
situation. There was nothing left for the missions to do than to go
home as quickly as possible.

In the interview published in the Soviet press on August 27,
1939, the head of the Soviet military mission described in the
following way the reasons for the failure of the military negotiations:

'The Soviet military mission considered that the U.S.S.R.,
having no common frontier with the aggressor, could give
assistance to France, Britain and Poland only on condition that
its forces were given passage through Polish territory, for no
other ways exist for the Soviet forces to enter into contact with
the forces of the aggressor. . . .

'In spite of all the obvious correctness of such a view, the British
and French military missions did not agree with this view of the
Soviet mission, while the Polish Government openly declared
that it did not need, and would not accept, military aid from the
U.S.S.R. . . .

1. Ibid., p. 119.

'In this lies the basis of the differences. And it was on this that the negotiations broke down.'

Replying further to a journalist's question—was it true, as stated by Reuters, that the Soviet Government had broken off the tripartite negotiations in view of its conclusion of an agreement with Germany?—the head of the Soviet delegation said:

'The military negotiations with Britain and France were not broken off because the U.S.S.R. had concluded a Pact of Non-Aggression with Germany. On the contrary, the U.S.S.R. concluded the Pact of Non-Aggression with Germany as a result, among other things, of the circumstance that the military negotiations with France and Britain had entered an impasse, in consequence of insurmountable differences.'[1]

This put all the dots over the 'i's.

1. *Pravda*, August 27, 1939.

Conclusion

THE most important conclusions to be drawn from the preceding pages are these

1. During the years before the war covered by these recollections (1932–9) the Soviet Union sincerely and persistently strove for the best possible relations with Great Britain. This was dictated, on the one hand, by its general policy of peace and peaceful coexistence with States based on a different system from that of the U.S.S.R., and on the other by the practical political calculation of the Soviet Government that together with Britain and France a reliable barrier could be brought into existence against the aggression of the Fascist Powers in Europe—Germany and Italy.

2. Unfortunately, however, the good wishes of the Soviet Union did not meet with a sympathetic response in Great Britain. True, there were many elements in the country—the workers, considerable sections of the intellectuals, the more far-sighted representatives of the bourgeoisie—who sympathized with the idea of creating a triple barrier against the Fascist aggression which threatened Britain herself and her world interests. But the State during the period described was firmly in the hands of the most reactionary strata of the bourgeoisie, for whom class hatred of the U.S.S.R. as a land of Socialism blotted out everything else. The leading political centre of this was the so-called Cliveden set which gathered in the drawing-room of Lady Astor, while their generally recognized leader was Neville Chamberlain. On account of its extreme hostility to the Soviet Union, the Cliveden set was resolutely opposed to the creation of a triple barrier for the defence of Britain's interests against the Fascist aggressors, and hit upon what seemed to it the happy idea of bringing about a conflict between Germany and the U.S.S.R., with the aim, once both these Powers had been bled white in an exhausting war, of

dictating to Europe a peace advantageous to Great Britain. Gradually gathering force, this foolish and criminal conception reached its peak after 1937, when Neville Chamberlain became Prime Minister and Lord Halifax Foreign Secretary. From this conception which inspired the Cliveden set there followed the policy of appeasement of the aggressors of Hitler in the first place; and in order that such a policy should be successful (an aim which after all was never achieved) Britain and France, with the support of particular circles in the U.S.A. in 1938 and 1939, sacrificed Austria, Spain and Czechoslovakia.

3. In spite of such unfavourable conditions, the Soviet Union nevertheless continued its efforts to improve its relations with Britain, and in 1939 to set up a barrier to Germany and Italy in the form of a triple pact of mutual assistance, seeing in this the best guarantee against Fascist aggression. In fact it was precisely the U.S.S.R. which took the initiative in proposing such a pact. The Cliveden set, although strongly opposed to such plans, found itself under pressure from wide sections of British public opinion and from some foreign States, which particularly feared Hitler and Mussolini: and in consequence was obliged to manœuvre, and to make believe from time to time that it was ready to take the path of creating such a triple barrier against the aggressors.

This manœuvring assumed its most pronounced character in 1939 after Hitler had torn up the Munich agreement. Hence followed the granting to Poland, Rumania and Greece, in March and April, 1939, of unilateral guarantees by Britain (and France) in the event of their being attacked by the Fascist States. Hence also followed the necessity for the Chamberlain Government (and likewise the Daladier Government) of taking part in the tripartite negotiations for the conclusion of a pact of mutual assistance with the U.S.S.R. But these were negotiations undertaken against their will, under the lash so to speak, in order to deceive the masses: and consequently they amounted in practice to pure sabotage, examples of which have been abundantly produced in the preceding pages. The chief concern of Chamberlain (and of Daladier) was not to strive for the conclusion of the triple pact as rapidly as possible but to find ways and means of avoiding its signature. The inevitable consequence of such a line of conduct on the part of the British (and French) Governments was that in August, 1939, the tripartite negotiations finally reached an impasse. It became quite clear that the creation of a truly effective triple barrier against the Fascist aggressors was becoming impossible owing and only owing to the sabotage of Chamberlain and Daladier.

4. Since the best form of resistance to the aggression of the Fascist States had become, in spite of us, unattainable, the Soviet Union had to think of other means of assuring its security, even though this assurance would be temporary and unstable. The great Lenin, in the first months after the October Revolution, had displayed his genius in a model manœuvre on the international arena. Striving to ensure that Soviet Russia, only recently born, should have the 'breathing space' which at that time it needed most of all, Lenin began by offering all the belligerent Powers the conclusion of a general democratic peace without annexations and indemnities. Lenin considered this to be the most desirable way of securing for the Soviet Republic a 'breathing space' which might become even a prolonged period of peace. But when it became clear that the appeal of the Soviet Government had fallen on stony soil Lenin decided that a separate peace with the German coalition should be concluded. This was, as Lenin called it, an 'obscene' peace, extremely unfavourable for Soviet Russia: nevertheless, it did provide her with a temporary 'breathing space' and, as subsequent events showed, was historically entirely justified.

Remembering this notable political example, the Soviet Government decided to follow it. Of course, circumstances and conditions in 1939 were somewhat different from those prevailing twenty-two years before, and first and foremost in the tremendous increase in strength of the Soviet Union: yet nevertheless in the world situation of 1939 there were not a few elements which made it akin to the situation in 1917–18. It was necessary at any price to prevent the creation of a single capitalist front against the U.S.S.R.; and it was vital, if not ultimately to prevent, at least to postpone for as long as possible an attack by the Fascist Powers on our country. This was dictated by the elementary feeling of self-preservation inherent in any State, irrespective of its nature. But it was also dictated by considerations of a more general character.

The Soviet Union at that time was not simply one of the great Powers existing on our planet. The Soviet Union represented something much more important: it was at that time the only country in the world which was the fatherland of Socialism, and which bore within itself the embryo of the Communist future of all mankind. On the shoulders of Soviet people at that time, and particularly on the shoulders of the Soviet Government, devolved the greatest responsibility for preserving the integrity and independence of a country so exceptional in its historical significance. The greatest responsibility demanded also the greatest courage, flexibility and resolution.

5. In the middle of August, 1939, the Soviet Government finally reached the conclusion that the policy of Chamberlain and Daladier excluded any possibility of signing a triple pact, and it decided to change its policy by ending negotiations with Britain and France as purposeless, and to conclude an agreement with Germany. Our adversaries abroad put into circulation the slanderous legend that in the spring and summer of 1939 the Soviet Government had been playing a double game—carrying on public negotiations with Britain and France for a triple pact of mutual assistance against the aggressors, and behind their backs secretly discussing a friendly agreement with Germany—and that in the long run it preferred Germany to the western democracies. In order to prove these malignant inventions the State Department of the U.S.A. even published in 1948 a particularly tendentious selection of German diplomatic documents captured in Germany by the Americans. But the detailed analysis of these documents for the period of the tripartite negotiations, which has been made in earlier pages, can leave no doubt whatsoever that such assertions are completely false. On the contrary, right up to the middle of August, and in spite of the crying sabotage of the tripartite negotiations by the governments of Britain and France, the U.S.S.R. continued to be their completely loyal partner, and

rejected all the attempts by Germany, of which there were not a few, to drive a wedge between the U.S.S.R. and the western democracies. But when, in the middle of August 1939, the Soviet Government came to the conclusion that it was quite hopeless to continue the tripartite negotiations, it decided to change its line of policy, and really did change it. In doing so it used the legitimate right of any Government to change its line of policy, should circumstances compel it to do so. In this particular case the change was all the more justifiable because it was imposed on the Soviet Government by the stupidly criminal behaviour of Chamberlain and Daladier.

6. The Soviet-German agreement of August 23, 1939, was, of course, not an act of perfection—and the Soviet Government never regarded it as such. But at any rate it did avert the possibility of the creation of a united capitalist front against the U.S.S.R., freed 13,000,000 western Ukrainians and Byelorussians from the terrible fate of becoming slaves of Hitler, ensured the national re-union of all Ukrainians and Byelorussians into single nations advancing rapidly on the path of Socialist development, and pushed forward the Soviet frontiers several hundred kilometres to the west, which was of great strategic importance. As later events showed, this agreement postponed the German attack on the U.S.S.R. for nearly two years, substantially facilitated the defence of the main centres of the country and then the victorious counter-offensive of the Soviet armed forces, made possible the destruction of Hitlerite Germany and ensured the preliminary conditions for the more rapid restoration of the strength of the U.S.S.R. in its present frontiers.

*   *   *

As a postscript, I want to quote here from the statements of two men who belong to opposite camps.

On November 27, 1958, N. S. Khrushchov addressed an extensive Note to the then President of the U.S.A., Dwight Eisenhower, in which he touched upon the world situation as it existed on the eve of the last war.

'It is common knowledge that it was not by any means immediately,' Mr. Khrushchov wrote, 'that the United States, or the United Kingdom and France either, drew the conclusion that it was necessary to establish co-operation with the Soviet Union with the aim of resisting Hitler aggression, though the Soviet Government constantly displayed readiness for this. In the capitals of the western States opposite tendencies prevailed for a long time. . . .

'It was only when Fascist Germany, upsetting the short-sighted calculations of the inspirers of Munich, turned against the western Powers, and when the Nazi army began moving westward, crushing Denmark, Norway, Belgium and the Netherlands and breaking the back of France, that the governments of the United States and the United Kingdom had no alternative but to acknowledge their miscalculations and take the road of organizing, jointly with the Soviet Union, resistance to Fascist Germany, Italy and Japan. Given a more far-sighted policy on the part of the western Powers, such co-operation between the Soviet Union, the United States, the United Kingdom and France could have been established much earlier, in the first years after Hitler seized power in Germany, and then *there would have been no occupation of France, no Dunkirk and no Pearl Harbour* [my italics—I.M.]. In that case it would have been possible to save the millions of human lives which were sacrificed by the peoples of the Soviet Union, Poland, Yugoslavia, France, Britain, Czechoslovakia, the United States, Greece, Norway and other countries in order to curb the aggressor.'

Winston Churchill, touching in his war memoirs on the tripartite negotiations of 1939, writes:

'There can be no doubt, even in the after-light, that Britain and France should have accepted the Russian offer. . . . But Mr. Chamberlain and the Foreign Office were baffled by this riddle of the sphinx. When events are moving at such speed, and in such tremendous mass as at this juncture, it is wise to take one step at a time. The alliance of Britain, France and Russia would have struck deep alarm into the heart of Germany in 1939, and *no one can prove that war might not even then have been averted* [my italics—I.M.]. The next step could have been taken with superior power on the side of the Allies. The initiative would have been regained by their diplomacy. Hitler could afford neither to embark upon the war on two fronts, which he himself had so deeply condemned, nor to sustain a check. It was a pity not to have placed him in this awkward position, which might well have cost him his life. If, for instance, Mr. Chamberlain on receipt of the Russian offer had replied: "Yes. Let us three band together and break Hitler's neck", or words to that effect, Parliament would have approved, Stalin would have understood and history might have taken a different course. . . . Instead, there was a long silence while half-measures and judicious compromises were being prepared.'[1]

In spite of all the differences between the authors of these two quotations (and I do not need to prove that they are very great) they are united in their opinion that the second world war could have been averted if the U.S.S.R., Britain, France and the U.S.A. (and at least the U.S.S.R., Britain and France) had rapidly, firmly and resolutely created an effective barrier against the aggresson of the Fascist States.

Who prevented the formation of such a barrier? The Soviet Union? No, the Soviet Union is not guilty of this. On the contrary, the Soviet Union did all that was humanly possible to bring the barrier into existence. What has been written in these pages should not leave the least doubt about this. The formation of the barrier in reality was prevented by the Cliveden set in Britain and the '200 families' in France. And if we are to speak of the persons who helped Hitler, who most completely embodied these reactionary forces and most actively applied the policy which suited them, we have in the first place to name Neville Chamberlain and Daladier. It is difficult to over-estimate all the depth of their historic responsibility for the launching of the second world war and for the innumerable sacrifices, losses and sufferings which it brought mankind.

---

1. *The Second World War*, Vol. I (1948), pp. 284–6.

Index of Names

DATE DUE